# Cooking with the
# Firehouse Chef

# Cooking with the
# Firehouse Chef

Keith Young FDNY Ladder-156

HPBooks

Cooking with the Firehouse Chef
Published by Kaley Young

Copyright © 2003
Text design by Richard Oriolo
Cover design by Ben Gibson
Cover photo by Jerry Ruotolo

John Sineno's Famous No-Bake Rice Pudding reprinted with the permission of Simon & Schuster Adult Publishing Group from *The New Firefighter's Cookbook* by
John Sineno. Copyright © 1996 by John Sineno.

FIRST EDITION: October 2003

This book has been cataloged by the Library of Congress.

PRINTED IN THE UNITED STATES OF AMERICA
9 7 8 0 5 7 8 4 2 7 2 4 9

# Dedication

I'd like to dedicate this book in the memories of FF Richard T. Muldowney Jr., L-7, and FF Patrick J. Boylan III, L-7.

Richie was a good friend of mine. I have wonderful memories of hanging out at his bay house, "Little America," and all the fun we had there. I remember the great

**Richie Muldowney, L-7**

time we had at Dave Weiss's (Rescue 1; died on September 11, 2001) bachelor party and being his roommate in Tampa, Florida, before his brother Timmy's wedding. I remember the way Richie would raise one eyebrow, growl, bark at me like an attacking pit bull, then give me a big hug and a kiss on the cheek. I get a big smile on my face whenever I think of him.

As far back as I can remember, all Richie wanted from life was to be a firefighter. It was in his blood, and he always called it the greatest J-O-B on earth. I still remember the day he told us he was being sworn in as a New York City firefighter. We were hanging out at E-216, his volunteer firehouse in Freeport. He was so proud, and we were proud of him. Richie knew exactly what he wanted to do for the rest of his life, and that's what he did. We lost Richie on September 11, 2001, along with 342 of New York City's Bravest. Richie and the rest of our heroes will never be forgotten.

Patty Boylan was Richie's good friend and the FDNY liaison to the Muldowney family after September 11, 2001. Patty worked tirelessly to help Richie's widow, Connie, and their two children deal with everything and anything that came their way in the wake of the disaster. He was always at the Muldowney family's disposal, and he helped not only them but every other family who lost someone from the firehouse. I knew him only a few months, but I felt as if I'd known him my entire

COURTESY ENGINE 16/LADDER 7

**Patty Boylan, L-7**

life. He was one of the nicest, most generous and sincere people I've ever met.

Patty eulogized his good friend Richie Muldowney on April 13, 2002. He died six days later, April 19, 2002, on the operating table during what should have been routine surgery. Patty's death was a terrible shock to all of us who knew him. It was as if someone had just thrown salt in our unhealed wounds. We will not forget you either, Patty.

# Acknowledgments

The road I've traveled from just a regular firefighter who happens to be a chef to the author of a cookbook has been long, exciting, and often surprising. It seems like I've just kept running into people who took me one more step on my journey, and I'd like to thank every one of them.

First of all there was Jerry Ruotolo, who's been with me since September 12, 2001, and who gave me his valuable time and the gift of his wonderful photos to include in this book. I would also like to thank Jerry's son, Rob, for all his help.

Then there's my friend Ted Harrington, who owns Ted Harrington Stationers and was going to help me self-publish this book—until a couple other lucky meetings sent me in another direction. Ted hired a mutual friend named Chip Moynihan to work with him. Then a woman named Meg Bowles came onboard. Meg asked Chip if he knew of any firefighters who might want to talk to a roomful of people on the subject "*Carpe Diem, a Time I Felt Most Alive*," and Chip volunteered me. Meg called, I said yes, and that one decision literally changed my life. I thought I'd be speaking to about 40 people, but it turned out to be an informal group called "The Moth," who get together periodically to tell and listen to stories. I was in a smoke-filled bar with more than 350 people, a stage, lights, and television cameras. I started to sweat. It was a terrifying but awesome experience, and one I'll never forget.

In the audience that night—October 24, 2001—were Jamie Raab, the publisher of Warner Books, and Amy Gross, senior editor at *O: The Oprah Magazine*. There was a brief biography of each of the speakers in the program, and mine said that I was working on a cookbook. Both women wanted to know more about it.

*O* magazine sent a wonderful writer named Susan Chumsky to my firehouse and published her article about me.

Jamie Raab somehow got my e-mail address and wrote that she'd like to see a proposal for the cookbook. I didn't even know what a proposal was, but Meg introduced me to a friend named Alexis Brunner, who happened to have been a cookbook editor. She's now the director at Discovery Kids Programming, but at the time she was between jobs, and her help with my proposal was instrumental in getting this book moving in the right direction and getting it published.

Then Alexis and Meg helped me find my tireless literary agent, Renée Zuckerbrot, who in turn introduced me to Judy Kern, who helped me rewrite the proposal and then worked with me on the book. And Meg is now working with me to produce a pilot for a television cooking show.

Meanwhile, back at the firehouse, Phil Scafuri, E-276, had a friend named Pat Campisi who worked at a publishing house, which turned out to be Putnam. (It's a small world because Pat's husband, Frank Campisi, L-107, a great guy, was one of my instructors at probie school.) "Anyway," Philly said, never one to shrink from giving advice, "Pat says you should talk to John Duff about getting this thing published. And don't be stupid about it. Strike while the iron is hot, 'cause they could lose interest in you real quick."

As it turned out, I was lucky enough to have three publishers interested in the book, but John Duff won me over with his enthusiasm and commitment to the project.

So that's pretty much the story of my wild and wonderful ride.

I'd also like to thank all the firefighters, members of my family, and my friends who have contributed their recipes to my book. My thanks to firefighters Bill Katsch, L-19, Vinny Mattone, E-319, Bobby Vazquez, E-212, Jimmy Mulligan, L-156, and Mike Henry and Paul Nicolosi, both promoted to lieutenant out of L-156, for their recipes. And a special thank you to Damian Ricardella, E-321, for all his desserts. Bill Katsch and John Miscanic, E-276, and his wife Jill were also kind enough to let me use their photos. I'd like to thank John Sineno, E-58 retired, for taking time out of his day to talk to me about the history of cooking in the firehouse, his rice pudding recipe, and his support. Unfortunately, John passed away on April 2, 2003.

I'd also like to thank all the guys in all the firehouses I've ever cooked in—E-319 in Middle Village, Queens; E-50, L-19, Bn-26 in the South Bronx; and my own house, E-276, L-156, Bn-33, Midwood, Brooklyn—for letting me cook and make lots of mistakes on you guys.

Thank you to my friend Dave "Dirtball" McAndrews for all the years he pressured me to take the FDNY test and get on the job.

Thanks to the FDNY, because if it weren't for this job my book would never have happened.

And finally, special thanks to my parents, Frank and Joan Young, and to my grandfather, Paul Munoz, for all the love, support, and help they have given me over the years. I also must thank my in-laws, Betty and Brendan King, for taking over when my mom passed away and for being great role models, not just for me but also for my children. They were always there whenever I needed them. I hope I have made all of them proud, and I want to let them know how much we miss them.

I've also got to thank my sisters and brothers, Mary, Laura, Duane, and Jeffrey, for putting up with me for all these years, and also all my brothers- and sister-in-law for dealing with me.

Last, but not least, I thank my wife, Beth, and my children, Kaley, Christian, and Keira, our latest addition, for being so understanding and helpful these past few years. I couldn't have come this far without all of you. I hope this book becomes a great success so I can make up for some of the time I couldn't spend with you when I was working on recipes for the cookbook or working at the firehouse.

I am a lucky man, and I'm thankful for everything I have in my life. Thank you all for helping me along the way!

Now, let's get cooking!

# Contents

# Introduction

We firefighters never know what our day is going to bring—it can be fighting a fire, but it can also be answering a false alarm, an EMS call, or dealing with an overturned car or an elevator that's stuck. Some days are slow, others are busy; some days are full of fun and fooling around, others are sad and somber. But no matter what we're called on to do, and whatever the mood, the one thing that's certain is we've got to eat—and eat well.

The people you work with in the firehouse are like your family, and like most families, the one time we have to get together and relax is during meals. Sometimes my "family" sits with me in the kitchen while I cook, drinking coffee and shooting the breeze. Or sometimes they leave me alone, which is okay, too. Cooking helps me clear my head when I'm in a bad mood or when I've had a rough day. It's also a good time for me to think about how quickly my kids are growing up and what I can do to improve their lives without making mine miserable. For me, the simple act of cooking can turn a rotten day into a pretty good meal, and that's not bad at all.

One day that even the comfort of cooking couldn't turn bad to good was September 11, 2001. I remember that it was clear and sunny and warm and that it was the first day of pre-kindergarten for our son, Christian. He and our daughter, Kaley, were all smiles that morning, and Christian was particularly proud of his new backpack. My wife and I walked him to the bus along with Kaley and our two dogs. We took lots of pictures of them both and then Christian's bus pulled up. Suddenly his big blue eyes turned all scared and nervous and I got a little teary, but my wife told me to "just let him go," so we hugged and kissed him and took another picture of him through the window and off he went.

After that we walked Kaley to her bus stop, and after waving her off with more hugs and kisses, my wife and I walked home. I remember feeling how lucky I was to have such a family.

Shortly after we arrived home, there was a phone call from my wife's nephew, Rob Volpe, who's a volunteer fireman in the town where we live. The first tower of the World Trade Center had just been hit, and he told us to turn on the television. I was watching with my wife and mother-in-law when the second plane hit. My wife was in tears and my mother-in-law just didn't know what to do. All I could think of was how much black smoke there was and how were they going to get up there and put the fire out? I knew I'd be losing someone I knew that day. I was pacing around nervously, practically sick to my stomach.

When the first tower came down, I said to my wife, "We just lost 200 men. I'm going to have to go in." She cried and begged me to not to, but I told her I had to go, it was my job. Then my lieutenant, Bill Howley, called. He said he thought we'd lost the Brooklyn Battery Tunnel and that I had to come in.

My wife wouldn't let me leave without seeing the children, so first we waited for Christian's bus. He was only in school half a day, so by that time he was on his way home. Then we went to pick up Kaley, who was, of course, delighted to be getting out early. I took both kids for ice cream and got them two scoops instead of the usual one. Then I told them that something bad had happened and I had to go to work. Kaley asked me when I'd be coming home, and I told her I didn't know; I'd be home as soon as they let me. I told them both to take care of their mother and grandma and be good to each other. They promised and we got in the car, but they started fighting and I started yelling at them and my wife started yelling at me, telling me I was being too tense and should try to calm down. I couldn't wait to get to work.

Driving on the Belt Parkway, usually one of NYC's busiest, in the middle of the afternoon, there was hardly another car in sight. It was the eeriest feeling I've ever had. When I finally arrived at the station, my lieutenant told me I wouldn't be going to the World Trade Center site because he needed me to stay in Brooklyn. The only apparatus left was the brush-fire unit. I tried to argue with him, but it didn't do any good. I was stuck and totally frustrated.

Cooking is the only thing that kept me sane during those dark hours. There were about twenty volunteers from New Jersey at the station along with our regular quota of thirteen men. Altogether, I fed about 40 guys. It kept me busy and at least I felt I was contributing something. As the night turned to early morning, some of our guys began straggling back from Manhattan. They were exhausted, their eyes were swollen and bloodshot, and they were completely covered in dust. At 3 A.M. I went upstairs to get some rest. I just tossed and turned.

The following morning, the chief told everyone who had been there overnight to go home and get some sleep because we'd have to come back the next day for a 24-hour shift. My friend Stevie Orr, E-276, and I got in the car and drove straight to Manhattan. When we got to the site, the devastation was almost unbelievable. There were at least two inches of dust covering everything, debris all over the place, and thick smoke still coming out of the buildings. The two of us just started working. We did things that day I hope we'll never have to do again in our lifetime. We were all hoping for a miracle, just to find any survivors. We worked until that evening before going home exhausted. When I got home, I hugged my wife and kids like I never had before.

Every single firefighter lost someone he or she knew that day—a brother fire-fighter, a sibling, a best friend. Some best friends died together.

That November, Brian DiFusco, L-156, and I decided to run the New York City Marathon in honor of the friends we had lost. We met up with Brian's friends Will Downey, L-103, and Brian Gallo, L-24. None of us had really trained, so when we were hurting and wanted to give up, the thought of our friends kept us going. We all crossed the finish line together.

If there's one good thing that came out of the unspeakable disaster of September 11, it was my meeting Jerry Ruotolo, who took many of the photographs for this book.

On September 12, I was working at ground zero with a group of men when we discovered a body and a dust-covered photograph on top of it that was completely intact. The picture was of a chef, several young women, and another man, and I assumed it must have belonged to the victim we found. There was a phone number

JERRY RUOTOLO

I found this photo at the World Trade Center site. Michael Lomonaco, center, was the executive chef at Windows on the World and this photo had been pinned to his bulletin board in his office.

**Standing with Brian Gallo, L-24 (left), Will Downey, L-103, and Brian DiFusco, L-156, before running the New York City Marathon in November 2001**

written on the back, so I folded the photo in half and put it in my pocket, thinking I could call the number and possibly assist the man's family in some way.

When I got home and showed it to my wife, she insisted that we call the number immediately, so she made the call and left a message.

The following day while I was working, my wife received a return call from Jerry Ruotolo, the photographer whose number was on the photograph. He was so happy we'd found the picture that he insisted on driving to our house right away to retrieve it. As they were chatting, my wife told Jerry I was working on a cookbook, and he told her he was a food photographer and wanted to help me with the book. He also told her the picture had been taken for a wine-tasting party and that everyone in it, including the chef, Michael Lomonaco, who was the executive chef at Windows on the World, the restaurant at the top of the World Trade Center, was alive and well. So in spite of the horror and devastation, I managed to pull something really nice out of the pile that day.

# Cooking with the Firehouse Chef

# Appetizers

I don't always make appetizers at the firehouse, but when we have the time I like to make something my brothers can munch on while I'm preparing the main meal, and it's also nice to have a snack that's both healthier and tastier than a bag of corn chips.

All the recipes in this chapter have been approved by my cohorts. They're easy and just as good for a barbecue, a cocktail party, or before a sit-down dinner at home as they are for feeding firefighters.

# Bruscetta

Bruscetta is usually served raw and cold over toasted Italian bread or garlic toast, but I like to sauté the onions and garlic to take out some of the bite and blend the flavors more rapidly. I make it when red, ripe tomatoes are in season and serve it warm.

SERVES 4 to 6   PREPARATION TIME 15 minutes   COOKING TIME 10 minutes

1 large loaf Italian bread

½ cup extra-virgin olive oil

1 Bermuda onion, diced

6 cloves garlic, minced

2 pounds ripe tomatoes, diced into ½-inch cubes

20 leaves fresh basil, chopped

Balsamic vinegar, to taste (optional)

Salt and freshly ground black pepper, to taste

½ cup freshly grated Locatelli Romano cheese

1. Preheat the broiler (to low if your broiler has two settings).

2. Slice the bread ½ to ¾ inch thick, arrange the slices on a sheet pan, and toast under the broiler until it turns golden, approximately 2 minutes on each side. Set the toast aside. Heat the olive oil in a large sauté pan over medium-high heat, then add the onion and sauté until translucent, 5 to 6 minutes. Add the garlic and sauté 2 more minutes. Remove the pan from the heat and add the tomatoes, basil, balsamic vinegar (if using) salt, and pepper to taste. Mix the ingredients gently and spoon the mixture over the toast. Sprinkle with the Romano cheese and return to the broiler for 30 seconds to color the cheese. Serve immediately.

# Garlic Bread with Gorgonzola Cream Sauce

**This sauce is about as simple and decadent as you can get. I tried it for the first time drizzled over a stack of garlic bread at a steak house, and I gobbled it up. The sauce is slightly greenish, so some people might not want to try it . . . all the more for you.**

SERVES 4    PREPARATION TIME 5 minutes    COOKING TIME 10 minutes

I cup heavy cream

6 ounces Gorgonzola cheese, crumbled

I recipe Garlic Bread (recipe follows)

In a medium saucepan over medium heat, combine the cream and Gorgonzola and stir gently until the cheese melts into a sauce. Remove it from the heat immediately and drizzle over the garlic bread, or serve it on the side and let people dip.

# Garlic Bread

**I use this same butter every year when we eat steamed lobster on my wife's birthday.**

2 tablespoons butter

2 tablespoons olive oil

3 cloves garlic, minced

I teaspoon dried oregano

I teaspoon chopped fresh parsley

Salt and pepper, to taste

I large loaf Italian bread or I long French baguette, sliced in half lengthwise

In a medium saucepan over medium-high heat, melt the butter and olive oil together. Add the garlic and cook for about 2 minutes until golden. Add the oregano, parsley, salt, and pepper, and spoon the mixture evenly over both sides of the Italian bread. The garlic bread can either be placed under a broiler, cooked open-faced until golden, or wrapped in aluminum foil and baked in a 350-degree oven for 5 to 10 minutes.

# Clams Casino

I love clams and I love bacon, so any recipe that combines the two has to be a favorite of mine.

SERVES **4**   PREPARATION TIME **40 minutes**   COOKING TIME **10 minutes**

**2 dozen littleneck clams**

**½ cup water**

**½ cup dry white wine**

**7 slices bacon, chopped**

**½ onion, finely diced**

**½ red bell pepper, finely diced**

**½ green bell pepper, finely diced**

**6 cloves garlic, minced**

**I teaspoon dried oregano**

1.  Preheat the oven to 350 degrees.

2.  Scrub the clams with a brush under cold running water. Put the clams, water, and white wine in a large sauté pan with a lid. Cover the pot and set it over high heat. As the broth boils, keep checking to see if the clams are opening. As they open, transfer them to a baking pan. When all the clams have opened, drain the leftover liquid from the pan to its own bowl. Do not wash the pan. Discard the tops of the clam shells. Add the bacon to the pan in which you cooked the clams and set it over medium-high heat. When the bacon starts to crisp, add the onion, red and green bell peppers, garlic, and oregano and sauté for 6 to 7 minutes, until the vegetables are soft. Add the reserved liquid from the clams and spoon the bacon and vegetable mixture over the clams and bake in the preheated oven for 8 to 10 minutes. Serve immediately, while they're still hot.

Appetizers

**That's me trying to grab a piece of bacon before it's all gone** JESSICA MAGNUSEN

# Clams Oreganata

These clams are as good as any I've ever eaten in a restaurant, if I do say so myself. If you don't like whole clams, chop them and double the topping recipe.

SERVES 4   PREPARATION TIME 15 minutes   COOKING TIME 10 to 12 minutes

**FOR THE TOPPING**

½ cup plain breadcrumbs

¼ cup freshly grated Romano cheese

2 cloves garlic, minced

I tablespoon chopped fresh parsley

I teaspoon dried oregano

¼ teaspoon salt

3 tablespoons extra-virgin olive oil

**FOR THE CLAMS**

2 dozen little-neck clams

½ cup dry white wine

½ cup cold water

2 tablespoons butter

2 tablespoons extra-virgin olive oil

I lemon, cut into wedges, for garnish

1.  Combine all the ingredients for the topping in a mixing bowl and set aside.

2.  Scrub the clams with a brush under cold running water.

3.  Preheat the oven to 350 degrees.

4.  Combine the white wine, water, butter, and oil in a large sauté pan or skillet with a lid and set it over high heat until the butter melts. Add the clams, cover the pan, but check the clams periodically and as soon as they begin to open, remove them to a bowl. When all the clams have opened, drain and reserve the juices left in the pan. Remove and discard the tops of the clam shells. Transfer the clams to a baking dish and spoon the topping over

them. Bake in the preheated oven for 10 minutes, or until the topping is golden brown and crispy. Transfer the clams to a serving platter, and spoon the pan juices over them. Garnish with the lemon wedges and serve. *Mmmm mmmm!*

## Keith's Confession

You have no idea how hard it is for me to admit this, but . . . I'm really bad at opening fresh clams with one of those clam knives. I've just never gotten the knack, and when I was working at a seafood restaurant, every time I was asked to do the raw bar, I managed to gouge my hand. So about 15 years ago, I threw away my clam knife and devised this method, which works for any dish *except* raw clams on the half shell. If you're eating yours raw, you'll either have to learn to open them yourself or eat them in a restaurant.

For any other clam dish, combine equal parts dry white wine and water in a large skillet, add the scrubbed clams, cover the pan, and steam the clams open over high heat. Keep checking and remove them to a bowl as they open. If they haven't all opened in 6 to 7 minutes, give the stubborn ones a good rap on the shell with tongs or a spoon, and if they still refuse to open, throw them away.

Now, examine the open ones for freshness. The clams should be plump, opaque, and whitish-gray in color. They should smell like fresh clams, slightly salty. If you find any that are yellowish-green, shriveled, or that smell like low tide, throw them away. Using even one less-than-fresh clam will compromise not only the dish but also your health, and, believe me, taking the chance just isn't worth it.

# Chopped Baked Clams with Fresh Herbs

**You can prepare these clams up to the baking point early in the day and refrigerate them, or freeze them for up to a week, then simply defrost and bake them.**

SERVES **4**   PREPARATION TIME **30 minutes**   COOKING TIME **10 minutes**

**2 dozen littleneck or cherrystone clams, scrubbed and rinsed**

**½ cup white wine**

**½ cup water**

**2 tablespoons olive oil**

**2 tablespoons butter**

**2 stalks celery, finely diced**

**½ onion, finely diced**

**12 cloves garlic, minced**

**1 teaspoon dried oregano**

**1 teaspoon finely chopped fresh parsley**

**½ teaspoon finely chopped fresh rosemary**

**½ teaspoon finely chopped fresh thyme**

**1½ cups crumbled saltine crackers or plain breadcrumbs**

**Salt and freshly ground black pepper, to taste**

**Paprika, for garnish**

1. Preheat the oven to 350 degrees.

2. Scrub the clams under cold running water. Place the clams, wine, and water in a large skillet. Set over high heat and cover the pan. Check the clams periodically and remove them as they open. Transfer them to a bowl and set them aside to cool.

3. In a clean frying pan, heat the olive oil and butter over medium-high heat. When the butter has melted, add the celery, onion, and garlic and sauté until the onion and celery are translucent, 5 to 6 minutes. Remove from the heat and set aside to cool.

Appetizers

4. Remove the clams from their shells and chop them roughly. Don't forget to save the shells. Transfer the chopped clams and their juices to a mixing bowl. Add the oregano, parsley, rosemary, thyme, and crackers or breadcrumbs, then add the onion mixture and salt and pepper to taste. Combine gently but thoroughly.

5. Fill the clamshells with the mixture and lay them on a sheet pan, sprinkle with paprika, and cook in the preheated oven for 12 minutes. Serve hot.

# Braised Clams in a White Wine Butter Sauce

**This dish is so quick and easy that it's a great firehouse dish. I love these clams either as an appetizer or as a main course served over linguine. The best part is the delicious broth made from the clams' juices. Take a fresh piece of Italian bread with a little bit of butter on it and dip it in the savory juice . . . it's *soooo* good.**

SERVES 3 to 4 as an appetizer or 2 as a main course over linguine

PREPARATION TIME 30 minutes   COOKING TIME 15 minutes

2 dozen littleneck clams

¾ cup white wine

¾ cup water

6 large cloves garlic, chopped

2 tablespoons butter

2 tablespoons olive oil

Salt, to taste

2 teaspoons dried oregano

1 tablespoon chopped fresh parsley

Juice of ½ lemon

½ teaspoon crushed red pepper flakes

1.  Scrub the clams with a brush under cold water.

2.  In a large sauté pan or skillet with a lid, combine the white wine, water, garlic, butter, olive oil, salt, and oregano and cook over high heat until the butter melts. Strain and rinse the clams and place them one by one in the pan, cover, and as the broth boils, check the clams periodically and remove only the open ones. After 7 or 8 minutes, rap the shells that don't open with a spoon. If they still don't open, throw them away. When all the clams have opened, add the parsley, lemon juice, and red pepper flakes to the broth. Taste it. It should be perfect.

3.  Return the clams to the broth to reheat for a minute or so. Serve them immediately with fresh bread, with or without linguine. *Bon appetit!*

# Ceviche

There is nothing more refreshing than fresh seafood. Ceviche is actually "cooked" by the acid in the marinade, so if you don't have impeccably fresh scallops, don't even bother to try it. The first time I ate this was on vacation in Cancun, Mexico. Now, every time I make it I'm reminded of beautiful beaches, lots of margarita, and the good time we had.

SERVES 4 to 5     PREPARATION TIME 15 minutes     MARINATING TIME 30 minutes

1 ½ pounds impeccably fresh sea or bay scallops, rinsed and roughly chopped

Juice of 2 to 3 limes juiced (about ½ cup)

2 tablespoons olive oil

½ medium red onion, diced

2 medium tomatoes, diced

2 tablespoons fresh cilantro, chopped

1 tablespoon chopped fresh parsley

1 ½ teaspoons kosher salt

½ teaspoon crushed red pepper flakes

1.  In a large mixing bowl, gently combine all the ingredients and refrigerate for 30 minutes before serving.

2.  You can serve this over a bed of lettuce or with nacho chips. Don't forget the margaritas!

# Garlic Ginger Teriyaki Shrimp

**The first time I prepared these shrimp, I was going to my friend Kris's house for his daughter's christening. I wanted to make a tasty, easy recipe that would feed about 30 people, a few shrimp per person. I didn't know that my friend Kris didn't eat seafood. But he must have liked what he smelled, or else he hadn't eaten in a few days, because he was popping these shrimp in his mouth one after the other. Anyway, the 5 pounds of shrimp I'd prepared for 30 guests fed the first 10 people at the party; the rest of the guests just heard about how good they were from Kris. Since then, I've made them at the firehouse a few times, and the guys eat them just as fast as Kris did.**

SERVES **4**   PREPARATION TIME **25 minutes**   COOKING TIME **12 to 15 minutes**

> 2 pounds medium shrimp, uncooked, in their shells
>
> ½ cup teriyaki sauce
>
> ¼ cup light soy sauce (50% reduced sodium)
>
> ¼ cup chopped, fresh cilantro
>
> ¼ cup sesame oil
>
> 12 cloves garlic minced
>
> ½ cup peeled minced ginger
>
> 1 to 2 teaspoons Tabasco sauce (depending how spicy you like the marinade)

1.  Preheat the oven to 400 degrees.

2.  Peel the shrimp but leave the final tail section on. Devein and partially butterfly the shrimp (butterfly just the area farthest from the tail so the shrimp will sit properly in the casserole dish). Set shrimp aside. Combine the remaining ingredients in a mixing bowl. Add the shrimp to the marinade and marinate for just about 5 minutes—any longer and the shrimp will be too salty.

3.  Remove the shrimp from the marinade and stand each one in a casserole dish, one behind the other, with each tail resting on the shrimp in front of it. Pour the marinade into the casserole dish, covering the shrimp by approximately ⅛ inch. Cook in the preheated oven for 10 to 12 minutes, until the shrimp are cooked through. Pull them out of the oven and enjoy.

**Getting ready to serve Garlic Ginger Teriyaki Shrimp**

# Deviled Crabby Patties

I admit that I don't make these at the firehouse very often, but I do often order crab cakes when I'm eating out. Sometimes they are excellent, and sometimes they're just okay. I believe these are a lot better than okay. The Ritz crackers give the cakes a rich and unique flavor, but you can also use the same quantity of saltines or breadcrumbs.

MAKES 6 to 7 (3-inch) cakes    PREPARATION TIME 20 minutes    COOKING TIME 20 minutes

1 pound lump crabmeat, picked through to remove any shell fragments

$\frac{1}{2}$ cup crumbled Ritz crackers

1 egg

$\frac{1}{4}$ cup finely chopped scallion, both white and green parts

$\frac{1}{4}$ cup finely diced red bell pepper

2 tablespoons mayonnaise (I prefer Hellmann's.)

1 tablespoon Dijon mustard

1 teaspoon Tabasco sauce

1 $\frac{1}{2}$ teaspoons Old Bay seasoning

2 cloves garlic, minced

Freshly ground black pepper, to taste

3 to 4 tablespoons olive oil

$\frac{1}{2}$ cup flour

Lemon wedges, for garnish

Deviled Mayo (recipe follows)

Gently fold together all the ingredients except the flour, olive oil, lemon wedges and Deviled Mayo, and form the mixture into six 3-inch patties. Heat the olive oil in a large cast-iron skillet over medium-high heat. Gently dredge the patties in the flour, turn them to coat all sides, and shake them very carefully to remove any excess. Cook the patties in the hot oil, in batches if necessary, for approximately 3 minutes on each side. They should develop a wonderful, golden-brown crust. Serve these delicious morsels immediately, with lemon wedges and Deviled Mayo, or with tartar sauce, if you prefer.

Appetizers

# Deviled Mayo

½ a cup mayonnaise (I prefer Hellmann's.)

¼ cup chopped dill pickle

1 teaspoon Tabasco sauce

Juice of ¼ lemon

Combine all the ingredients in a small bowl and serve with the crab cakes.

# Eggplant Rollatini

This is a good recipe to make in large quantities, either at the firehouse or for parties. You can freeze the leftovers or refrigerate and eat them over the next several days. When I make it at the firehouse, however, there usually aren't any leftovers.

Serves 12 to 15   PREPARATION TIME 30 minutes   COOKING TIME 25 minutes

2 cups extra-virgin olive oil

3 large eggplants, thinly sliced lengthwise

2 cups flour

9 eggs, beaten

3 pounds ricotta cheese

1½ pounds mozzarella cheese, grated

2 cups freshly grated Romano cheese

3 cloves garlic, minced

⅓ lb prosciutto, thickly sliced and diced

¼ cup chopped fresh parsley or basil

Salt and freshly ground black pepper, to taste

1 recipe My Marinara Sauce (page 133)

1. Preheat the oven to 350 degrees.

2. Fill a large skillet with olive oil to a depth of about ¼ inch and set it over medium-high heat. Dip the eggplant in the flour and then in the beaten egg. When the oil is hot enough for a bit of flour to sizzle when it's dropped in, fry the eggplant in batches for about 2 minutes on each side, until it's lightly browned. Transfer the slices to a sheet pan as they're done, and keep adding a bit more oil to the pan as needed. In a large mixing bowl, combine the ricotta, ⅔ the mozzarella, ½ the Romano, the garlic, prosciutto, parsley or basil, and salt and pepper to taste. Place about 1 tablespoon of the mixture at one long end of an eggplant slice, roll it up, and transfer it, open side down, to a baking dish large enough to hold all the eggplant in a single layer. Repeat this process with the remaining eggplant and filling. Cover the rolled eggplant with the marinara sauce, sprinkle with the remaining mozzarella and Romano, and bake in the preheated oven for 25 minutes or until hot. Serve immediately.

Appetizers

# Helping Out

Sometimes when we're cooking in the firehouse, certain guys take offense if someone isn't helping out in the kitchen. When that happens they usually find some way to get back at the one who isn't pulling his weight.

One time Doug Price, E-276, was so engrossed in one of FDNY's procedural handbooks (hard as that may be to believe) that he didn't realize everyone around him was working on the meal, which happened to be eggplant Parmesan heroes. At some point, Bobby Eichele, L-156, realized that after the eggplant was breaded and fried it resembled a Dr. Scholl's shoe insert. You know what happened next. The guys found a couple inserts, which they breaded and fried. Then they carefully sauced and cheesed the inserts and placed them on a hero roll. They looked good enough to eat.

The boys picked up their meals and then called Dougy to come get his. Dougy picked up his sandwich, sat down to bite into it, but then decided to cut it in half. At that point, of course, he realized that his eggplant was blue on the outside and black on the inside. The guys had been hoping he'd just take a big bite, but things at the firehouse don't always go the way you plan them.

# Spicy Brooklyn Wings

**It seems as if just about everybody claims to make the "best-tasting, spiciest chicken wings." All I know is that I like to eat chicken wings and I don't have all day to spend making the hot sauce. This recipe is a relatively quick and easy way to make them without sacrificing any of the taste.**

SERVES 6   PREPARATION TIME **20 minutes**   COOKING TIME **20 minutes**

**5 pounds chicken wings**

**2 quarts peanut or vegetable oil**

**2 cups flour**

**1 (23-ounce) bottle Frank's Hot Sauce or another brand of your choice\***

Cut the chicken at the joints, discarding the outermost bony portion of the wings (or save them for a stock). Rinse the wings, dry them on paper towels, and set them aside. Heat the oil in a large stockpot over medium-high heat. Be very careful and *always stay with your stove whenever you are frying anything! Remember, this is a fireman talking.* Dredge the chicken wings in the flour, shake them to remove the excess, and add them to the pot in small batches so the temperature of the oil remains constant. Fry until they are golden brown and the meat starts to pull away from the bone, about 4 to 5 minutes. Remove the chicken wings from the hot oil with a slotted spoon and transfer them to a large mixing bowl. Preheat the broiler. Gently stir in enough hot sauce to evenly coat the wings. Arrange the coated wings in a single layer and crisp them for 1 to 2 minutes under the hot broiler. Serve with bleu cheese dressing, carrot sticks, and celery sticks.

*Appetizers*

\*I like Frank's because it's medium-hot, but if you like your wings a little less spicy, coat them with equal quantities of Frank's Hot Sauce and Open Pit BBQ sauce.

**With Sara Moulton after a "Cooking Live" Superbowl
Party segment. We made Spicy Brooklyn Wings and
Garlic Ginger Teriyaki Shrimp**

JERRY RUOTOLO

My friend Dave "Dirtball" McAndrews, E-289, and my mother-in-law, Bette King,
at the 2001 Ronzoni Pasta Party

Appetizers

# Spicy Sautéed Chicken Livers and Chicken Hearts

I used to make this dish with just chicken livers until my best friend and childhood buddy, Dave "Dirtball" McAndrews from E-289, suggested that I add the hearts. I don't know why, but I listened to him, and to tell you the truth this is the first time listening to him didn't get me into trouble. The hearts give the dish a totally different and unique texture. So the next time you're in a restaurant and the waiter tells you the "blue plate special" has chicken hearts in it, don't be afraid to try it. Or by all means, make this dish for yourself.

SERVES 6 to 8    PREPARATION TIME 25 minutes    COOKING TIME 10 minutes

I pound chicken livers

I pound chicken hearts (If you don't want to use hearts, double the quantity of livers.)

3 tablespoons olive oil

I large onion, diced

9 cloves garlic, diced

I fresh jalapeño pepper, diced

½ teaspoon crushed red pepper flakes

¾ teaspoon kosher salt

3 tablespoons chopped fresh parsley

Rinse the chicken livers and hearts. Remove the fatty yellow portion at the top of the hearts, dice the hearts, and place them in a bowl. Discard any livers that look yellow or greenish. A healthy liver should be a deep brownish-red. Remove the fatty connective tissue between the livers, dice the livers, and add them to the bowl with the hearts. Heat the oil in a cast-iron skillet and sauté the onion until it is translucent. Add the garlic and jalapeño pepper and sauté for about 30 seconds. Next, add the livers and hearts and sauté for 5 to 6 minutes over a medium to high heat. Add the crushed red pepper and the salt. When the mixture is fully cooked, add the parsley and serve. The boys at the firehouse like to eat this with crackers or toasted bread.

# Stuffed Mushrooms

Stuffed 'shrooms are a favorite around my house for holiday parties because they're so easy and quick to make.

SERVES **4 to 5**   PREPARATION TIME **20 minutes**   COOKING TIME **15 to 20 minutes**

1 tablespoon olive oil

½ onion, diced

3 cloves garlic, minced

1 pound sweet Italian sausage, casing removed

1 cup shredded mozzarella cheese

½ cup freshly grated Romano cheese

½ cup plain breadcrumbs

1 tablespoon chopped fresh sage

1 teaspoon dried oregano

Salt and freshly ground black pepper, to taste

2 pounds button or cremini mushrooms, stems removed

1. Preheat the oven to 350 degrees.

2. In a skillet over medium-high heat, heat the oil and sauté the onion and garlic until translucent, about 5 minutes. While the onion and garlic are sautéing, thoroughly combine the sausage, mozzarella cheese, Romano cheese, breadcrumbs, sage, oregano, and salt and pepper. When the onion and garlic are done, add them to the stuffing mixture and mix thoroughly. Set the mushroom caps upside down on a cookie sheet and fill them with the stuffing. Bake in the preheated oven for 15 minutes and check one to make sure the stuffing is completely cooked through with no pink sausage. If not, return them to the oven for a few more minutes before serving.

Appetizers

# Fresh Guacamole

Serve this dish as an appetizer with corn chips or as a condiment for tacos and wraps. Just don't make it more than two hours before serving, because the guacamole will turn brown.

SERVES 5 to 6    PREPARATION TIME 10 minutes

3 ripe avocadoes, peeled, pitted, and cubed

Juice of 1 lime

½ red onion, finely diced

1 to 2 cloves garlic, minced

1 teaspoon chopped fresh jalapeño pepper (or more if you like it spicy)

3 tablespoons chopped fresh cilantro

1 tomato, diced

Salt and freshly ground pepper, to taste

In a bowl, thoroughly combine all the ingredients except the tomato until the mixture is like a paste. Add the tomato, gently mixing, and taste the guacamole. If necessary, adjust the seasoning with more salt and pepper or more jalapeño until it's to your liking.

## When the Alarm Goes Off

The alarm has absolutely no respect for our need to "refuel." If a call comes in when we're cooking or eating, we all have to stop whatever we're doing and jump on the rigs. We hope that someone will remember to turn off the stove before we leave the building. Having a fire in your own firehouse could be rather embarrassing. It hasn't happened to me, but I did hear a story when I was working in the Bronx about firefighters who forgot to shut off the gas and returned to find a three-alarm blaze at their station.

# Homemade Hummus

My wife can eat this entire recipe in one sitting as a meal with some fresh raw veggies or good tortilla chips. Use it as a sandwich spread, as in Beth's California Pita Sandwich with Hummus (page 59), or as a dip. This recipe is basic; you can create your own flavorful variations—or try Beth's favorite, below.

MAKES ABOUT 2 cups    PREPARATION TIME 5 minutes

1 (15½-ounce) can chick peas

¼ cup juice reserved from chick peas

¼ cup extra-virgin olive oil

1 to 1½ tablespoons fresh lemon juice

1 clove garlic, chopped

½ teaspoon salt

½ teaspoon ground cumin

Freshly ground black pepper, to taste

In a food processor or blender, combine all ingredients and pulse on low speed until thoroughly mixed, then blend on high speed for about 1 minute. Taste to make sure the hummus is smooth and flavorful. If necessary, adjust the seasonings with more salt, pepper, and/or lemon juice. You can eat it immediately or chill it in the refrigerator for ½ hour before serving.

VARIATION  This is my wife's favorite: Substitute lime juice for the lemon juice and add approximately 2 tablespoons fresh cilantro and fresh jalapeño pepper or crushed red pepper to taste.

Appetizers

# My Tomato Education

In the spring of 2002, I took an excellent cooking class given at Grace's Market on the Upper East Side of Manhattan by cookbook author and culinary educator Micol Negrin. Before the class started, she led us through the market and explained how and why she chose each of the ingredients she was going to use in her recipes. When she started talking about tomato products, I learned something.

I asked her what makes some canned tomato products taste better and less acidic than others. Were some tomato products simply inferior? Her answer was that the more acidic, less flavorful tomatoes were packed with citric acid as a preservative. So now I know that if I want to be sure my sauce is as flavorful as possible, I should look for tomatoes that don't contain this ingredient. The sauce won't require any added sugar, and it won't have to cook as long to compensate for the acid.

Then she introduced me to a product I had never tried before—Pomi brand tomatoes, which are packaged in Italy in waxed airtight boxes. The ingredients read "Tomatoes," period. I suggest you try them. They're great for both sauces and salsas.

And always remember to read the ingredients on everything you buy, canned or otherwise. It's important to know what you're eating.

# Spinnin' Salsa

Serve this with chips as an appetizer or use it as a condiment with tacos or wraps. The salsa can be prepared a day in advance and refrigerated until serving.

SERVES 4 to 5   PREPARATION TIME 15 minutes

4 cups diced ripe tomatoes or 1 (26½-ounce) box Pomi brand chopped tomatoes or 1 (28-ounce) can whole tomatoes, with their juice, hand crushed

1 cup diced red onion

1 fresh jalapeño pepper, diced

2 tablespoons chopped fresh cilantro

2 cloves garlic, minced

2 teaspoons kosher salt

Juice of ½ lime

Combine all the ingredients thoroughly in a large bowl and taste the salsa. You can adjust the seasoning or quantities of various ingredients to suit your taste. When you're happy with it, it's ready to go.

Appetizers

# Soups

I love both cooking and eating soups. They're hearty, warming, and filling, and they always remind me of my mother's kitchen. Whether creamy and smooth like the Cream of Country Vegetable or chunky with good things to chew like the Pasta Y Fagioli, soups are always a big hit at the firehouse, and they really make the whole place smell great.

I like to make my own stock, so I've included recipes here in case you'd like to try it. But if you don't have the time or the inclination, you can always start with canned stock from the supermarket. Try for low-sodium, though, because most commercial stocks are very salty and can affect the balance of flavors in the other ingredients.

# Beef Stock

**The neck bones of the beef are perfect for making a stock. The neck has a lot of flavor because these are the muscles used most frequently, and the bones are also inexpensive. There's no reason to use a tender, expensive cut of meat for making a stock.**

MAKES APPROXIMATELY ½ gallon    PREPARATION TIME 45 minutes
COOKING TIME 2 to 3 hours

   4 pounds beef neck bones

   4 quarts cold water

   I bay leaf

   I teaspoon whole peppercorns

1.   Preheat the oven to 400 degrees.

2.   Place the beef bones in a roasting pan and roast them in the preheated oven for about 30 minutes, until they turn a deep brown. Transfer the bones to a saucepot or stockpot. Add some cold water to the pan and scrape off all the drippings with a wooden spoon. Add that water to the pot along with the 4 quarts cold water. Add the bay leaf and pepper-corns. Gently bring the ingredients to a slow simmer, skimming frequently. Let the stock simmer for 2 to 3 hours.

3.   Strain, and save the meat from the bones to garnish the broth.

Soups

# Depression Chicken Stock

**This is the kind of stock your mother or grandma might have made during the Great Depression in the 1930s. I enjoy making stocks like this for soups because they use every part of the chicken. Nothing goes to waste; I think that's very important. Normally, when you make a chicken stock, you use carrots, celery, onions, peppercorns, bay leaf, fresh herbs, and maybe even a whole chicken. To me, boiling a whole chicken and all those vegetables is a waste. First of all, you remove most of the flavor from the meat, then you discard the veggies, then you put other vegetables into the soup. I like to eat a roast chicken, or make chicken salad or chicken potpies, and save the bones for making stock. This works really well at home but not so well at the firehouse. Start the stock with chicken parts if you are working at a firehouse.**

MAKES APPROXIMATELY ½ gallon    PREPARATION TIME 3 minutes
COOKING TIME 2 hours

**Leftover bones from 3 or 4 roasted chickens including the drippings from roasting, or about 3 pounds chicken parts (Fowl is excellent to use for stock because it's older and has a deeper chicken flavor.)**

**3 quarts water**

**I bay leaf**

**I teaspoon whole peppercorns (optional)**

Combine all the ingredients in a large pot and gently bring to a slow simmer, skimming frequently. Let the stock for simmer for 2 hours. It should reduce by about ⅓; if it reduces more, add a bit more water. Carefully strain the stock into another pot and discard the bones, bay leaf, and peppercorns. You should have about ½ gallon. Now you are ready to make soup.

VARIATION **To make turkey stock, use one turkey carcass. Crush the chest cavity so all the bones are covered with water. Use it to make any recipe that calls for chicken stock.**

# Depression Ham Stock

This is made virtually the same way as the chicken stock. I use smoked pork neck bones, but you can also use a leftover smoked ham bone. It's really easy, and the stock gives your soup a wonderful smoky flavor.

MAKES about 2 quarts    PREPARATION TIME 5 minutes    COOKING TIME 2 hours

3 quarts cold water

2 to 3 pounds smoked pork neck bones (you can get these at the supermarket), a smoked ham bone, or smoked ham hocks

1 bay leaf

1 teaspoon whole peppercorns

Combine all the ingredients in a large pot and gently bring to a slow simmer, skimming frequently. Simmer for 2 hours. The liquid will reduce by about ⅓. Remove from the heat and strain the liquid carefully into another pot. Remove the meat from the bones and save as a garnish. Discard the bones.

# Beef, Mushroom, and Barley Soup

**This is an absolutely great recipe to serve at the firehouse or your own house on a cold and blustery afternoon, although it's actually hearty and filling enough to serve for dinner. I like to serve this soup with nice thick, crusty pieces of bread with lots of butter.**

MAKES 8 to 10 (8-ounce) servings    PREPARATION TIME 20 minutes
COOKING TIME 45 minutes to 1 hour

2 tablespoons extra-virgin olive oil

1 onion, finely diced

2 cloves garlic, minced

1 carrot, finely diced

1 celery stalk, finely diced

1 parsnip, finely diced

10 to 12 ounces white mushrooms, sliced (or any mushroom of your choice)

2 quarts beef stock, homemade or store-bought

¾ cup barley

Salt and freshly ground black pepper, to taste

1 tablespoon freshly chopped parsley

Optional garnish: shredded meat from beef bones if stock is homemade

In a large soup pot, heat the oil over medium-high heat. Add the onion and sauté until translucent, about 5 minutes. Add the garlic, carrot, celery, parsnip, and mushrooms and sauté another 5 minutes. Next add the beef broth and barley. Bring the soup to a simmer and cook until the barley is tender, about 30 minutes, stirring occasionally so nothing sticks to the bottom of the pot. Season the soup with salt and pepper and stir in the parsley. Serve immediately, garnished with the shredded beef (if using).

# Black Bean Soup

Every time I make a dish with black beans in it, I'm reminded of my Puerto Rican grandfather. He was about 5' 4", but in the kitchen he was a giant in my eyes. Everything he made tasted great and smelled even better. I love to prepare food that takes me back to those days when he was around. Sometimes that's what cooking is all about.

MAKES **10 (8-ounce) servings**   PREPARATION TIME **20 minutes**
COOKING TIME **1½ to 2 hours for dried beans; 30 minutes for canned**

6 cloves garlic, peeled and roughly chopped

4 tablespoons olive oil

I large Spanish onion, diced

I green bell pepper, seeded and diced

I stalk celery, diced

2 teaspoons dried oregano

I tablespoon distilled white vinegar

3 sprigs fresh parsley or cilantro

½ gallon Depression Ham Stock (page 32)

I (16-ounce) package dried black beans, soaked, drained, and rinsed, or 4 (15-ounce) cans black beans

2 teaspoons Goya Adobo seasoning

Salt and black pepper, to taste

Chopped scallions, for garnish

Shredded meat from pork or ham bones, for garnish

1. When I make this in the firehouse, I like to cook the stock and soak the beans the night before. Once the stock is finished, I pick the meat off the pork bones and reserve it for garnishing the soup.

2. In a large pot, over medium-high heat, sauté the garlic in the olive oil until it's slightly golden brown. Add the onion, stir, and sauté for 2 minutes, then add the green bell pepper and celery. Sauté until the onion becomes slightly translucent and the peppers soften, about 5 minutes. Add the oregano, vinegar, parsley, ham stock, and beans. Slowly bring to a simmer and, cook until the beans start to soften, about 1½ to 2 hours if you are using the

Soups

dry beans. Black beans from a can are already soft and need to cook no more than ½ hour. If the mixture becomes too thick, add a little bit of water. When the soup is done, taste it and add the Adobo seasoning, salt and black pepper only if necessary. Purée the seasoned soup in batches in a blender. Make sure you fill the blender only halfway so the soup doesn't overflow. (This will save you a trip to the burn center.) Garnish with the chopped scallions and shredded meat, and enjoy.

3. This dish can also be served over rice as black beans and rice, in which case you should not purée the beans at all.

## Lieutenant Pepper Pocket

When I was in probie school, I heard all kinds of stories about all the pranks firefighters pull on the probies (graduates of the firefighters' training school). The first few weeks I was waiting for someone one to pull something on me, but the only prank I noticed was an extremely lame one. Someone kept dumping ground black pepper into my pocket, and it didn't me take too long to figure out who it was—one of the lieutenants in the engine—because he was about as smooth as a box of rocks. I actually caught him at it four or five times, but I never let on.

Eventually, it was payback time. One day the lieutenant came in the kitchen while I was cooking the meal. He was looking over my shoulder, trying to act interested in what I was making. I watched as he spilled pepper all over the floor in a feeble attempt to get some of it into my pocket. I was all ready for him. When he turned his back to leave, I sprinkled the cheapest, smelliest Parmesan cheese all over both his shoulders. He smelled like dirty feet for hours but couldn't figure out what it was or where it was coming from. Then I watched as he tried to brush the cheese off of his shoulder. This is when the smell really imbedded in his clothes. He eventually changed his shirt—and when he did I got him again.

# Butternut Bisque

When I created this recipe, I'd actually been thinking about making a pumpkin bisque, but pumpkin was not in season, so I decided to use butternut squash instead. I was also trying to re-create the exquisite cream of root vegetable soup I'd had at **DB Bistro Moderne** in Manhattan. This recipe was the happy result of my attempting to combine the two. I hope you enjoy it as much as my family and I did.

MAKES 12 (8-ounce) serving    PREPARATION TIME 15 minutes

COOKING TIME 45 minutes to 1 hour

2 quarts chicken stock, homemade or store-bought

1 (3- to 4-pound) butternut squash, peeled, seeded, and cubed

1 large (about 2-pound) yellow turnip, peeled and cubed

1 large onion, peeled and diced

1 parsnip, peeled and chopped

1 carrot, peeled and chopped

1 stalk celery, diced

3 whole cloves garlic, peeled

1 teaspoon allspice

1 cup heavy cream, hot (do not boil)

Salt and freshly ground black pepper, to taste

In a large saucepot or stockpot, bring the chicken stock, squash, turnip, onion, parsnip, carrot, celery, and garlic to a slow simmer. Then cover and cook for 45 minutes, stirring occasionally. Test the vegetables for doneness by mashing a piece with a fork. The turnips will probably take the longest to cook. When all the vegetables are soft, transfer the soup to a blender in batches, filling the container no more than halfway, and purée it. Transfer the purée to another pot or bowl (not plastic) as it's done. Add the allspice, hot heavy cream, and salt and pepper to taste. Reheat if necessary before serving, but do not let it boil or the cream will curdle.

Soups

# Chicken Noodle Soup

This is my son Christian's favorite soup in the whole wide world. It reminds him of his grandma. He used to sneak down to her apartment with his sister, Kaley, to ask his grandma for his favorite soup, and my mother-in-law would instantly grant his wish by opening a can and serving it with a sandwich or toast. I like to make chicken noodle soup from scratch, just to get the kids to eat a bit healthier. My daughter likes it thickened slightly, so it's more like the soup Grandma served them.

MAKES 8 (8-ounce) servings    PREPARATION TIME 20 minutes    COOKING TIME 40 minutes

2 quarts chicken stock, homemade or store-bought

1 to 1½ cups diced chicken, reserved from making the stock or one 8- to 12-ounce chicken cutlet, cooked and diced small enough to fit on a spoon

1 onion, finely diced

2 carrots, finely diced

1 stalk celery, finely diced

2 cloves garlic, minced

2 cups 2-inch-long fine egg noodles

3 tablespoons cornstarch mixed with 3 tablespoons water (optional)

2 tablespoons chopped fresh flat-leaf parsley

Salt and pepper, to taste

Combine the chicken stock, chicken, onion, carrots, celery, and garlic in a large soup pot over medium-high heat. Bring the soup to a simmer and cook approximately 25 minutes. Add the noodles and bring the soup back to a simmer for about 5 minutes, until the noodles are cooked. With the soup at a medium simmer, stir in the cornstarch and water mixture (if using). Bring the soup back to a simmer and remove it from the heat. Stir in the parsley and salt and pepper to taste. Serve with crusty Italian bread and lots of butter.

# Cream of Country Vegetable Soup

I get a kick out of getting people to eat things they say they don't like without their knowing it. My daughter, like many other children, never really liked vegetables. My challenge was to get her to eat some veggies and to enjoy doing it. When she was three, I used to tell her this was cheese soup because she's quite a little cheese eater. It really isn't even a cream soup, because there's no cream in it; it just tastes like there is. In fact, it's virtually fat free, although it's so smooth and creamy that you'd never know it. If you have a problem getting your kids to eat their vegetables, try making this soup. Even my buddy Rob Angelone, E-276, loves it, and he won't eat a single vegetable.

MAKES APPROXIMATELY 8 (8-ounce) servings     PREPARATION TIME 10 minutes
COOKING TIME 30 minutes

2 quarts chicken stock, homemade or store-bought (for a vegetarian soup, use vegetable stock or filtered water)

1 to 1¼ pounds red potatoes, with their skins on, cubed

1 stalk celery, chopped into ½-inch pieces

2 carrots, cut into ½-inch pieces

1 onion, diced

3 whole cloves garlic, peeled

Kosher salt and freshly ground black pepper, to taste

½ cup freshly grated Romano cheese

Combine all the ingredients except the salt, pepper, and cheese in a large pot and slowly bring to a simmer. Cook, stirring occasionally, until the vegetables are soft and cooked through, about 30 minutes. Purée it in batches in a blender, filling the container no more than ½ full, and transfer the purée to a clean pot. If the soup seems too thick, stir in cold water, a little at a time, until it reaches the consistency you desire. Reheat it if necessary, season with salt and pepper, and serve garnished with the grated cheese. I hope you and your children enjoy this one.

Soups

# Lazy Lentil Soup

**Low in fat and high in protein, fiber, and complex carbohydrates, this is a complete healthy meal in a bowl.**

MAKES APPROXIMATELY **8 (10-ounce) servings**    PREPARATION TIME **10 minutes**

COOKING TIME **45 minutes**

> **2 quarts Depression Ham Stock (page 32), meat from the bones reserved**
>
> **1 cup cold water**
>
> **1 (16-ounce) bag dried lentils**
>
> **1 medium onion, diced**
>
> **3 cloves garlic, chopped**
>
> **2 carrots, chopped into ½-inch pieces**
>
> **1 stalk celery, chopped into ½-inch pieces**
>
> **Salt and freshly ground black pepper, to taste**
>
> **Fresh herbs of your choice, such as parsley, sage, rosemary, or thyme (optional)**

1.  In a large saucepot, combine all the ingredients except the salt, pepper, and fresh herbs. Slowly bring the soup to a boil, then lower the heat and simmer uncovered for approximately 45 minutes, stirring occasionally. Remove the soup from the heat and taste. Add salt, pepper, and fresh herbs and taste again. Don't overdo the salt, because once you've added it, you can't remove it.

2.  Lentil soup thickens naturally as it simmers and also when it is refrigerated. You can thin it, if necessary, to the consistency you desire by stirring in small quantities of cold water.

# Manhattan Clam Chowder

When I was a teenager, I worked in a seafood restaurant on the Nautical Mile in Freeport, New York, where the chef used to prepare this soup daily. I loved it, so I came up with my own recipe.

MAKES 8 (8-ounce) servings   PREPARATION TIME 30 minutes   COOKING TIME 45 minutes

3 dozen cherrystone or littleneck clams

1 cup dry white wine

1 cup water

6 slices bacon, diced

4 cloves garlic, minced

2 carrots, diced

1 stalk celery, diced

1 medium onion, diced

1 (28-ounce) can whole tomatoes, chopped in a blender

2 to 2½ cups reserved clam broth, plus additional water if needed

2 russet or Yukon gold potatoes, peeled and diced

2 teaspoons fresh thyme, or 1 teaspoon dried

½ teaspoon dried oregano

Salt and pepper, to taste

3 to 4 splashes Tabasco sauce

1. Place the clams in a large skillet with a lid, set over high heat, and add the white wine and water. Cover the pan, and, as the clams start to open, remove them and set them aside in a bowl. Re-cover the pan and repeat the process until all the clams have opened. Discard any that don't open after 7 or 8 minutes. Reserve the liquid in the pan and in the bowl. Remove the clams from their shells and dice the meat.

2. In a large sauce pot over medium-high heat, cook the bacon until it starts to brown. Add the garlic and stir. Let the garlic sauté for about 30 seconds, then add the carrots, celery, and onion, and sauté for another 10 minutes, until the vegetables soften. Add the tomatoes, reserved clam broth, clams, potatoes, thyme, and oregano and simmer for another 30 minutes or so, until the potatoes soften. Season with salt and pepper and a few splashes of Tabasco sauce. Serve the chowder with traditional oyster crackers.

Soups

# Pasta Y Fagioli

I always get a kick out of listening to people try to pronounce words that aren't native to their language. My sister-in-law Maureen calls this soup "Pasta Fazooh." The first time I heard her say it, I was at Sunday dinner at my in-laws' house, and everybody at the dinner table started cracking up. Maureen's said it quite a few times since then, and it still makes me smile.

For most soup recipes, I prefer to use fresh stock, but in this recipe, for the sake of convenience and time, you can use low-sodium, reduced-fat canned chicken broth.

**SERVES 8    PREPARATION TIME** 20 minutes    **COOKING TIME** 20 minutes

6 slices bacon, cut into ½-inch pieces (You could also use pancetta or prosciutto; just cook them with the onions and garlic.)

½ cup olive oil

6 cloves garlic, peeled and minced

I medium onion, diced (about 1½ cups)

4 (15½-ounce) cans white beans, in their liquid (Cannelini, great northern, or small white beans will do.)

I (28-ounce) can whole tomatoes, hand crushed or chopped in a blender

2 quarts Depression Chicken Stock (page 31) or 4 (15½-ounce) cans low-sodium, reduced-fat chicken broth

I pound small pasta (tubettini, orzo, elbows, orichiette, or small shells), cooked al dente

Kosher salt and crushed red pepper, to taste

½ teaspoon dried oregano

4 tablespoons chopped fresh parsley

I cup freshly grated Pecorino Romano cheese

In a large saucepot over medium-high heat, cook the bacon until slightly crispy. Drain the fat from the bacon, but do not clean the pot. In the same pot, heat the olive oil, add the garlic, and sauté until it turns golden. Add the onion, return the bacon to the pan, and sauté about 5 minutes, until the onion becomes translucent. Stir in the beans with their liquid, the tomatoes, and the chicken stock, and bring to a boil, then lower the heat and simmer for 5 minutes. Add the pasta, season with kosher salt and crushed red pepper. Stir in the oregano and parsley and serve immediately, passing the grated cheese on the side.

# Sausage and White Bean Soup

This is a healthy, stick-to-your-ribs kind of soup that I love to make at the firehouse in the fall and winter. If you prefer a spicy soup, use a half-pound hot sausage and a half-pound sweet. You can also garnish this soup however you like, with crumbled bacon, grated cheese, fresh croutons, or just some fresh chopped parsley. I prefer the ham stock for this recipe because it gives the soup a deep, smoky flavor.

MAKES approximately 10 (8-ounce) servings    PREPARATION TIME 30 minutes    COOKING TIME 3 hours

2 quarts Depression Ham Stock (page 32) or Depression Chicken Stock (page 31)

1 (16-ounce) package small white dried beans or 2 (15½-ounce) cans small white beans with their liquid

2 tablespoons olive oil

1 pound sweet Italian sausage, removed from its casing

1 medium onion, diced

2 carrots, roughly chopped

1 stalk celery, chopped

3 cloves garlic, peeled

3 new potatoes, cubed

Salt and pepper, to taste

1. While the stock is simmering, rinse and start cooking the dried beans, if using them. Place the beans in a pot of cold, unsalted water to cover the beans by at least double their depth. Bring to a boil, reduce the heat, and simmer covered for approximately 1½ hours or until the beans are soft.

2. In a second stockpot, heat the olive oil over medium-high heat and brown the sausage in the oil. When it has browned, add the strained stock, 4 cups soaked dried beans or all the canned beans with their liquid, the onion, carrots, celery, garlic, and new potatoes.

3. Bring to a boil, then lower the heat and simmer for approximately 30 to 45 minutes, until the vegetables are soft. When the soup is done, purée it in batches in a blender, filling the container only halfway to prevent the soup from overflowing and possibly scalding you. Pour the puréed soup into a clean pot to reheat. Season it with salt and pepper, and serve at once, garnished however you prefer.

# Cold Hard Cash

Most guys pay for their meals in U.S. currency. One of the guys from my friend Dave McAndrew's firehouse, L-138, E-289, isn't like most guys though.

One day John M. was detailed to another firehouse. To get there, he had to take a highway and pay a toll. These were the days before E-Z Pass, and he apparently used all the cash he had to pay the toll—or at least that's what he said. When the guys at the house he'd been detailed to that day asked if anyone was out on the meal, John M. never said a word—in fact, he ate as soon as it was served. When a voice came over the speaker system at the end of the meal and announced, "Five bucks a man. Pay up, deadbeats!" John went out to his car and returned to the kitchen with two quarts of 10W-40 motor oil. He said he figured each quart of oil was probably worth $2.50, so they were even.

# Lunch Stuff

Firefighters are always hungry, and some of the things I make for lunch—such as fried chicken, chili, and pizza—might make perfect dinners for most people. Feel free to serve them at whatever hour you choose; they'll be good at any time of the day or night.

People sometimes ask me whether the guys ever bring their lunch, and all I can tell them is that anyone caught "brown-bagging it" without a good excuse, such as a real dietary restriction, would catch so much flack from the rest of us for not participating in the communal meal that he'd probably never try it again—at least if he knew what was good for him.

# 10–75 Chili

FF Bobby Vazquez of E-212 in Brooklyn gave me this recipe. I was lucky enough to meet Bobby while I was on light duty at Division 11. We hit it off immediately. Other firefighters who were working with us could not stop bragging about what a good cook Bobby was. We started talking about food, one thing led to another, I told him I was writing a firehouse cookbook, and he gave me this recipe. This is the official winning recipe of the New York City Firehouse Chili Contest sponsored by Bloomingdale's, and it's a keeper. By the way, a 10–75 is FDNY's code for a working structural fire, so you might want to have a glass of water handy while you eat this chili.

SERVES 6 to 8    PREPARATION TIME 20 minutes    COOKING TIME 2 hours

2 pounds lean ground beef

1 pound sweet Italian sausage, skinned and crumbled

4 cups beef stock, fresh or canned

1 teaspoon saffron threads

3 tablespoons olive oil

2 cups coarsely chopped shallots

2 cloves garlic, minced

1 (10-ounce) can green chilies, drained and chopped to a rough purée

1 teaspoon oregano

1 teaspoon cumin

½ teaspoon cayenne pepper

2 tablespoons chili powder

1 teaspoon salt

Freshly ground black pepper, to taste

1 (6-ounce) can tomato paste

1 (15½-ounce) can kidney beans, drained (optional)

In a heavy skillet, brown the ground beef and the sausage. Transfer to a 4-quart pot. In the same skillet, bring the beef stock to a boil. Remove the stock from the heat. Crumble the saffron and add it to the stock. Add the olive oil to the skillet and cook the shallots and garlic for 5 minutes, stirring frequently. Remove from the heat and add the chilies, oregano, cumin, cayenne pepper, chili powder, salt, and a few grindings of black pepper. Stir to combine and then add the tomato paste and reserved beef stock. Mix thoroughly and add to the meat in the pot. Bring to a boil, stir, reduce the heat, and simmer partially covered for 1½ hours. Add the beans (if using) 10 minutes before the chili is done. Bobby likes to serve this over white rice, but you can also serve it in a bowl as is. Enjoy!

JOHN MISCANIC E-276

# Chili 1-2-3

This recipe is really quick and easy as well as low in fat and high in protein and fiber. It's filling, too, which is great for the guys at the firehouse. Even my kids love it as long as I don't make it too spicy.

SERVES 8    PREPARATION TIME 10 minutes    COOKING TIME 15 to 20 minutes

½ cup olive oil

I large onion, diced

I large green bell pepper, seeded and diced

9 cloves garlic, peeled, and roughly chopped

2 pounds very lean ground beef

4 (15½-ounce) cans Goya pink beans, with their liquid

I (28-ounce) jar good-quality tomato sauce or crushed tomatoes

2 tablespoons chili powder

I teaspoon ground cumin

I teaspoon dried oregano

½ teaspoon cayenne pepper, optional (use less or none if you don't like your chili too spicy)

Goya Adobo seasoning or salt, to taste

2 tablespoons chopped fresh cilantro

**SUGGESTED GARNISHES**

Chopped raw onion

Grated cheddar cheese

Sour cream

Chopped fresh jalapeño pepper, for those who like it really hot!

In a large saucepan, combine the olive oil, onion, and green bell pepper and sauté on medium to high heat until the onion becomes translucent and the pepper softens, about 5 to 7 minutes. Add the garlic and sauté another minute, then add the ground beef and brown, breaking the meat up with the side of a spoon, until all the redness is gone. Because the meat was very lean, there is no reason to drain it. Add the pink beans with their liquid and the tomato sauce. Bring the mixture to a simmer and season with the chili powder, cumin, oregano, and cayenne pepper. Season to taste with Adobo seasoning or salt and stir in the cilantro. Serve the chili over rice or a baked potato, if you wish.

# My Firehouse Cooking Debut

It was only my sixth tour of duty and I was still trying to make a good impression—trying to remember names, saying "Yes, sir" and "No, sir," and generally putting my best foot forward. The lieutenant on duty one day was a really nice guy, and when he asked me if I knew how to cook, of course, I said yes. I figured if I made something good for my new brothers I'd make a few friends.

It was pretty cold out, and he thought chili would be a good idea. When I looked in the fridge to see what we had on hand, I noticed a pot with some leftover red sauce. I asked one of the guys when they'd made it and he said the night before. Good enough! I wouldn't have to buy tomato sauce. So I got the rest of my shopping list together and we jumped in the truck and headed for the nearest supermarket. The guys were jumping all over me from the get-go, questioning every ingredient, second-guessing every item I put in the cart. That's a good sign, by the way, part of the camaraderie. If they aren't giving you a hard time, you know you're in trouble! Anyway, when we finally got to the checkout counter, my "brothers" had disappeared, so I had to pay for the food. A great start to a beautiful day.

Back at the firehouse, I set to work. They asked if I needed help and I said no, so they left me alone to do my thing. I diced and sautéed the vegetables, browned the meat, seasoned the chili, added the beans, and then poured in the red sauce. Here's where I made my big mistake: I added the sauce without tasting it first. *Never, ever do that!* I let everything cook for a few minutes and then tasted the chili. It tasted a bit "off" to me, but I couldn't quite put my finger on what was wrong, so I added a bit more salt and spices and tasted it again. The "off" taste was still there, but by that time the guys were getting restless, so I plated my food and yelled "Chow's up!" into the intercom. The guys were not only starving but also obviously curious to find out if I could really cook.

I'll never forget what happened next. The biggest guy at the table let out a shriek like a little girl who'd just seen a mouse, and says, "What are you trying to do, kill me? I'll die of ana-phylactic shock if I eat this s**t!" He lifted his spoon in my direction, and that's when I saw it—the large lower half of a calamari affectionately known as "spider legs."

The "sauce" from the night before was Seafood Fra Diablo.

One by one, they all dumped their lunch in the garbage. The only ones left eating were a cop from the neighborhood who'd dropped in for lunch and me.

Needless to say the next three hours, which I spent riding around on the rig doing building inspections with a bunch of really hungry and unhappy firefighters, were not the best of my life.

# Almost Kentucky Fried Chicken

**If you like fried chicken you can't help loving this recipe. It's so tasty that I can't stop nibbling on it. The buttermilk creates a thick coating that absorbs the flour to make the thick crust. The addition of Tabasco gives it just the right kick. Serve this dish at your firehouse or at a party with corn on the cob and fresh coleslaw, and I promise you, there won't be any leftovers.**

SERVES **4 to 5**   PREPARATION TIME **30 minutes**   MARINATING TIME **8 hours to overnight**
COOKING TIME **45 minutes**

2 whole (2½- to 3-pound) chickens

4 cups (1 quart) buttermilk

¼ cup Tabasco sauce

4 tablespoons Lawry's Seasoned Salt or McCormick Seasoned Salt

4 cups flour

Vegetable oil (about 2 cups) for frying

Kosher salt to taste

1. Rinse the chickens and cut them into eight pieces each, cutting the breasts into thirds, or have your butcher do it. Remove all the skin so the chicken will be less fatty and can absorb more of the flavor of the marinade.

2. Combine the buttermilk, Tabasco sauce, and Old Bay seasoning in a large bowl and whisk to combine. Add the chicken pieces and turn them to be sure they are well coated on all sides. Refrigerate, covered, for at least 8 hours or overnight.

3. Place the flour in a shallow dish, add the chicken pieces, and turn to coat them heavily on all sides. Arrange the coated chicken pieces, not touching one another, on a sheet pan and refrigerate for 45 minutes to allow the buttermilk to absorb the flour. Do not discard the flour remaining in the dish.

4. Preheat the oven to 350 degrees.

5. Fill a large cast-iron skillet with vegetable oil to a depth of about ½ inch and set it over medium-high heat. Before adding the chicken, sprinkle a pinch of flour in the oil. If the flour sizzles, the oil is hot enough. Re-flour the chicken and shake off any excess, then brown it in batches in the hot oil for 5 to 6 minutes on each side. Transfer the pieces to a

sheet pan as they're done. Don't overcrowd the pan or the chicken won't brown properly. When all the chicken has been fried, place the sheet pan in the preheated oven and cook for 20 minutes, or until the juices run clear when the chicken is pricked with a fork. Sprinkle with kosher salt and serve immediately. Put some aside for yourself, because it's going to go quickly.

## Firehouse Staples

**Almost any firefighter, even a brand-new probie, knows that there are certain things, like butter and milk, that you always "pick up" when you're procuring the meal.**

One morning, the guys at my firehouse asked one of the new guys to go out for butter and milk. They were having bagels and coffee, and they'd run short. So the probie left and returned a few minutes later with two quarts of buttermilk. One of the senior men took a look at it and said, "Whoa, what's this?" "Buttermilk," said the probie. "What you guys asked me to get." "What on earth would I want with buttermilk in the morning?" asked the senior guy. But the probie insisted. "I don't know, but that's what you guys told me to get." In fact, he was actually very annoyed with them. That's what the guys found so funny. Instead of just returning the buttermilk and not making a scene, the kid argued about it. You can rest assured that after that, they messed with him about picking up buttermilk every chance they got.

# French Bread Pizzas

**The guys at the firehouse love these. When I make them, I never have to worry about what to do with the leftovers because there aren't any. The beauty of these pizzas is that you can top each one differently to suit different tastes and cravings.**

**SERVES 4**  **PREPARATION TIME** 15 minutes  **COOKING TIME** 15 minutes

I cup **My Marinara Sauce (page 133), or your favorite store-bought brand**

I recipe **Garlic Bread (page 3)**

1½ to 2 cups **freshly grated mozzarella cheese**

I cup **freshly grated Romano cheese**

**Pizza toppings of your choice, precooked if necessary**

1. Preheat the oven to 350 degrees.

2. Spread just enough marinara sauce over the garlic bread to cover it lightly. Sprinkle with the cheeses, add your favorite toppings, and toast the bread in the preheated oven for approximately 10 minutes, until the cheese has melted nicely. Cut into individual serving pieces and serve while it's hot.

Lunch Stuff

# Mike "Squarehead" Henry's Barbecued Pizza

One thing about us firefighters—we have to be resourceful, think on our feet, and use whatever tools we have available to us.

One evening when I arrived at the firehouse to work the night shift I kept hearing the day guys talking about what a great pizza they'd had for lunch. The more they talked about it, the more I liked it—and I hadn't even tasted it yet. It had been a very hot day, and because the guys didn't want to heat up the kitchen, they'd picked up pizza dough from a local pizzeria and barbecued it outdoors on the grill.

As you might imagine, the grill at our firehouse isn't exactly state-of-the-art. In fact, it doesn't even have a cover, which might be why I burned three batches of dough trying to duplicate the barbecued pizza before I got it right. Unfortunately, I had a large audience to witness my culinary failure, and they haven't let me forget about it yet.

Pizza dough purchased from a pizzeria works best but the kind that's sold frozen in the supermarket is OK too. If you're grilling, use a pizza screen; in the oven, a pizza screen, a clay pizza dish, or a baking sheet all work well.

SERVES 2 to 3    PREPARATION TIME 10 minutes    COOKING TIME 20 to 25 minutes

1½ to 1¾ pounds uncooked pizza dough

Olive oil, for brushing the dough

Pinch of kosher salt

Pizza toppings of your choice

1 cup good-quality marinara sauce of your choice

2 cups freshly grated mozzarella cheese

1 cup freshly grated Pecorino Romano cheese

1. Clean the grill rack thoroughly, because any leftover debris will immediately be imbedded in your pizza dough. A pizza screen could be very helpful if your grill rack is hard to clean or slightly rusty.

2. Preheat the grill to medium-high (about 400 degrees). At home, I have a Weber grill with a built-in thermometer and fairly even heat, which make things a bit easier. I'm not telling you to go out and purchase a Weber grill, but they are pretty good. If your grill doesn't have a thermometer, you can place an oven thermometer inside the cover to see what the internal temperature is.

3. Shape the pizza dough with your hands to about ¼ inch thick. It can be a square, a rectangle, or a circle—whatever suits your fancy. I have a round pizza screen, so I make the dough fit the screen. Brush both sides lightly with olive oil and sprinkle the top with a pinch of kosher salt. Place the dough on the grill rack and cook covered for about 5 minutes, then rotate it 180 degrees to ensure even browning, cover, and cook another 5 minutes. After 5 to 6 minutes you should see bubbles forming on top and the dough shouldn't sag when you lift it. Turn it over. (Using a second pizza screen is the easiest way to do this, but if you don't have one, just lift it with your hands.) The cooked side should be a light golden brown. Spread it with the Marinara sauce and add the cheeses. Add toppings to the pizza if you'd like, cover the grill, and cook 6 minutes to melt the cheese and warm the sauce. Check periodically to be sure the bottom of the crust isn't burning. Rotate the pizza 180 degrees and cook another 5 to 6 minutes. Remove from the grill, slice, and enjoy. You will be amazed how thin, crunchy, and delicious the crust is.

Toppings like pepperoni or fresh basil can be added after the pizza has been sauced and cheesed, but sausages, ground beef, or meatballs should be precooked and added after the sauce and cheese.

Dedicated to the memory of Joseph Henry.

## Mike "Squarehead" Henry

His head doesn't look so square to me, but some of the other guys think he's a real boxhead, and Mike, good-natured guy that he is, has even posed for a picture with a box on his head. It's now on "the wall of shame," in the supermarket where we buy our food hangs photos of shoplifters. The guys think this is very funny.

Mike's kind of quiet, but he also loves to pull practical jokes. One of his favorite ploys is to stir up a little trouble for the new guys. When a new group of probies is about to report for duty, a department order goes out to all the fire stations listing their names and the firehouse where they'll be working. Before their first day of work, they all have to report to their commanding officer wearing their dress blues and traditionally toting a box of cake or pastry. The officer gives them their schedule and shows them around—a kind of orientation. What Mike loves to do is get his hands on the department order and call one of the hapless probie's officer at another station. His favorite time to do this is at 11 o'clock at night, when the officer is likely to be resting. Then, pretending to be the new recruit, he starts mouthing off, telling the officer that he'll be in the following morning, that he can't work that weekend, and generally giving him enough lip so that when the real probie actually shows up, he's certain to be starting the job with the officer already ticked off. (And yes, the unfortunate victim does start the job at something of a disadvantage, but it all gets straightened out in the end, and "sucking up" the hazing is just part of what it is to be among the brothers in New York.)

Another of Mike's tricks is to call the station where an officer has been newly promoted, pretending he's the new lieutenant calling down from the officer's room. He then instructs whoever answers that he doesn't eat bread and he doesn't eat pasta, and all he wants is plain meat, so that when the real lieutenant arrives for his first meal all he sees on his plate is a few slices of dry meat.

Mike himself was recently promoted to lieutenant and the guys in our house—his old house—didn't lose any time thinking of a way to give him a dose of his own medicine. As soon as he got to his new assignment after going through officer training school, John Miscanic, E-276, pulled one of Squarehead's old tricks on him. John phoned the department line at Mike's new station from our house and, pretending to be Mike calling from upstairs, told the person who answered to get all the junior guys together and start training on the Hurst Tool (the Jaws of Life). He also said he'd be down in a few minutes to see how things were going.

Half an hour later, one of the junior men went up to Mike's office, knocked on his door, and said, "We did what you asked. Are you going to be coming down soon?"

"What'd I ask?" Mike wanted to know, totally bewildered.

When the guy told him, he knew right away what was going on. They both laughed and then Mike phoned our house to see who had "gotten" him.

It's all part of the firehouse code, just another way the guys have of teasing those they'd give their lives for if called upon to do so.

JOHN MISCANIC E-276

Mike "Squarehead" Henry—who else?

# Marinated Lamb Kebobs with Yogurt Sauce

The first time I made this at the firehouse I brought the leg of lamb with me. But then I started to debone it and realized I really needed another one. The guys loved the dish, but they weren't too happy about having to go out and buy a second leg at the last minute.

Serve the lamb in a pita pocket with shredded lettuce and thinly sliced onions or over a bed of brown or white rice, with the tomatoes on the side. If you're using wooden skewers for this, be sure to soak them thoroughly in water so they don't burn on the grill.

SERVES 6   PREPARATION TIME ½ hour   MARINATING TIME 1 hour
COOKING TIME 10 to 12 minutes

### FOR THE SAUCE

1 pint plain yogurt

1 pint reduced-fat sour cream

1 cucumber, peeled, seeded, and diced

1 tablespoon chopped fresh parsley

Fresh ground black pepper, to taste

1 tablespoon Goya Adobo seasoning, or to taste

### FOR THE KEBOBS

Juice of 5 lemons

1 cup olive oil

12 cloves garlic, diced

4 tablespoons chopped fresh basil or cilantro or 2 tablespoons of each

2 teaspoons dried oregano

2 teaspoons cumin

Kosher salt and crushed red pepper, to taste

4 to 5 pounds boneless leg of lamb, cut into 1-inch cubes

1 green bell pepper, cored, seeded, and cut into 1-inch chunks (optional)

1 large Spanish or Vidalia onion, cut into 1-inch chunks (optional)

36 ripe cherry tomatoes

Lunch Stuff

1. Combine the sauce ingredients in a bowl and refrigerate until ready to serve.

2. In a large mixing bowl, combine the lemon juice, olive oil, garlic, basil or cilantro, oregano, cumin, salt, and crushed red pepper. Taste the marinade and, if necessary, adjust the seasonings to your taste. It should have a bit of a kick. Add the lamb, turning to be sure it's completely coated, cover, and marinate in the refrigerator for 1 hour.

3. Preheat the outdoor grill to high.

4. Skewer the marinated lamb cubes with the peppers and onions. Skewer the cherry tomatoes separately, about six to a skewer. Once the lamb has been skewered, turn the grill down to medium-high, 400 to 450 degrees, and place the kebobs on the grill. Grill for 10 to 12 minutes, turning the kebobs every 1 or 2 minutes to be sure the lamb browns on all sides and doesn't burn. When the lamb is done, grill the cherry tomatoes briefly, just until they color slightly and the skin begins to shrivel, about 1 to 2 minutes. Remove the lamb and tomatoes from the skewers and serve with the yogurt sauce.

# "Linner"

JERRY RUOTOLO

Captain Lake, L-156, with Stevie Orr, E-276

When I'm on duty at the firehouse, I'm usually the one who cooks, but just because they like what I make doesn't mean the guys don't give me a hard time about using more pans than anyone else (because they're the ones who have to clean up) and that my meals take too long to prepare.

Even my captain, Brian Lake, gets into the act. After one lunch—French dip sandwiches, French fries, and Timmy Boy's chopped salad—that didn't get served until 2 P.M. he pulled me aside to tell me eating at 2 P.M. wasn't lunch and it wasn't dinner. It was something in between. It was "linner." (I can't say that I think "linner" will catch on the way brunch—that odd meal between breakfast and lunch—has done, but for my own sake I'll try to set the trend.)

Lunch Stuff

# Beth's California Pita Sandwich with Hummus

This is probably my wife Beth's favorite sandwich, even though she's not a vegan. The first time she had it we were on vacation in Lake Tahoe. The weather was as beautiful as the scenery, so we ordered sandwiches for lunch and then picnicked on the beach by the lake. There we were, sitting on a sheet on the sand and looking at snow-covered mountains across the pristine lake. This sandwich reminds her of that awesome vacation.

**SERVES 2   PREPARATION TIME 20 minutes**

2 (8-inch) whole-wheat pitas

1 recipe Homemade Hummus (page 24)

½ large cucumber, peeled and sliced

1 avocado, peeled, seeded, and sliced

1 large ripe tomato, sliced

1 cup alfalfa sprouts

JERRY RUOTOLO

My wife, Beth, and I at the Buglisi Foreman Dance Company performance where I was guest of honor

Place the pitas on a cutting board and slice them in half so you have four semicircles. Open the semicircles and spread one side of each generously with hummus. Add 3 slices cucumber, 2 slices avocado, 2 slices tomato, and ¼ cup alfalfa sprouts, then top with the remaining hummus. Dive in. It's a little messy, but it's delicious and healthy.

# Bratwurst Sandwich

This is a quick and delicious lunch. I crave it especially in the cold winter months, although the guys don't seem to mind when I make it for them in the summertime.

SERVES 4　PREPARATION TIME 5 minutes　COOKING TIME 5 to 7 minutes

I (8-ounce) bag sauerkraut

8 bratwurst sausages, scored and sliced in half lengthwise

8 slices fresh rye bread

Spicy deli mustard or Dijon mustard

Dill pickles

1.　Heat the sauerkraut in a medium saucepan over medium heat.

2.　Place the bratwurst sliced side down, either on a preheated grill or in a skillet over medium heat. Brown it about 3 minutes on each side and remove from the heat. Spread 4 slices of bread generously with mustard. Cover each slice with 4 pieces of sausage. Add the warmed sauerkraut, cover with the remaining bread slices, and serve with dill pickles. I also like some good potato chips on the side.

VARIATION Instead of sauerkraut, use kimchi, a spicy, fermented Korean cole slaw. You don't have to heat the kimchi. This is actually my favorite way to make it, although I sometimes have a problem finding the kimchi.

Lunch Stuff

# Chicken Bruscetta Sandwiches

This is good, healthy stuff—high in protein with fresh vegetables to boot. This sandwich is a favorite at **The Highway**, the nickname for our firehouse located off King's Highway.

SERVES **4**   PREPARATION TIME **25 minutes**   COOKING TIME **20 minutes**

**FOR THE CHICKEN**

**2 pounds skinless, boneless chicken breasts, rinsed, trimmed, cut in half crosswise, and pounded**

**Salt and freshly ground black pepper, to taste**

**¼ cup olive oil**

**FOR THE BRUSCETTA**

**¼ cup olive oil (in the same pan the chicken was cooked in)**

**I Bermuda onion, diced**

**6 cloves garlic, minced**

**2 pounds ripe tomatoes, diced**

**20 leaves fresh basil, chopped**

**Salt and freshly ground black pepper, to taste**

**2 loaves Italian bread, split lengthwise, then cut in half crosswise**

**Balsamic vinegar, to taste**

**½ cup freshly grated Romano cheese**

TO COOK THE CHICKEN: Season the breasts with salt and pepper. Heat the oil in a large skillet, preferably cast iron, over medium-high heat. When it's hot enough that a pinch of flour sizzles when dropped in, add the chicken and cook approximately 2 to 3 minutes on each side, until it turns golden brown. Set the chicken aside on a sheet pan. Do not wash the pan.

TO MAKE THE BRUSCETTA: Preheat the broiler on high. Add the olive oil to the pan in which you cooked the chicken and set it over medium-high heat. When the oil is hot, add the onion and sauté until it is translucent, 5 to 6 minutes. Add the garlic and sauté for 2 more minutes. Remove the pan from the heat and add the tomatoes, basil, salt and pepper.

TO FINISH THE SANDWICHES: Reheat the chicken under the broiler for 1 to 2 minutes and then place 2 cutlets on each of 4 slices of bread. Top with the bruscetta mixture, drizzle with balsamic vinegar, sprinkle with grated cheese, and place under the broiler for 30 seconds to 1 minute. Top with the remaining bread and enjoy.

JERRY RUOTOLO

Lunch Stuff

# Grilled Chicken Club Sandwich

This sandwich is perfect for those times when you want to eat something that's basically healthy with just a little bit of decadence.

SERVES 5 to 6    PREPARATION TIME 20 minutes    COOKING TIME 30 minutes

3 pounds chicken cutlets, rinsed, trimmed, sliced in half widthwise, and pounded flat

½ cup olive oil

Salt and pepper, to taste

6 kaiser rolls

Mayonnaise

3 ripe tomatoes, sliced

1 head of red leaf lettuce, separated and washed

1 pound bacon, cooked and drained

1.  Preheat the gas grill on high.*

2.  Brush the chicken liberally with the olive oil, season with salt and pepper, and place them on the preheated grill. Cook, turning, until they are golden brown on both sides and the meat is white on the inside. Cut open the rolls, swipe a little mayo in there, a couple slices of tomato, some lettuce, some bacon, a couple chicken breasts, and you are good to go.

*If you don't have a grill, you can cook the cutlets in a pan on top of the stove.

# Buying Food and Cooking for the Firehouse

In New York City, we firefighters pay for our own meals. That's both good news and bad news. The bad news is that we pay for our meals; the good news is that we can eat whatever we want.

Once we've decided as a group what we're going to eat on our shift, the truck and the engine take turns going out to buy the food—or, to use the correct terminology, "procure the meal." One month it's the truck, the following month it's the engine, and so on. And just in case you didn't know the difference, the engine, or pumper, carries the hose and the truck, or ladder, carries the big ladder or bucket for the tower ladder that's raised on the outside of the building in case either firefighters or civilians have to leave rather hastily.

If you live in New York City, you might have seen firefighters shopping alongside you in your local supermarket. But don't worry, we're on duty even when we're shopping, and we always leave someone on the rig with a radio to let us know if there's an emergency.

JERRY RUOTOLO

The truck and I

Once the meal has been "procured," everyone lends a hand putting it together. When I'm on duty, however, most of the cooking generally falls to me. Not that I'm complaining, mind you. Cooking is something I really love to do. It's just that sometimes it's hard to get everyone to agree on what we're going to eat.

The guys on my shift are usually pretty good about letting me plan the menu, and they know that if, for example, I'm making fish, I'll also make some chicken for those who think fish belong in the water and not on the plate. But one particular brother, Frank Malone, E-276, whose favorite foods are chicken, bacon, and cheese, took some unwelcome initiative when the firehouse voted on tuna and pita bread for lunch. He came back from the market with chicken cutlets, hero rolls, American cheese, macaroni salad, potato salad, and potato knishes!

# Quick and Easy Chicken Cordon Bleu Hero with Mushroom Gravy

**This recipe saves a lot of calories and time in the kitchen without sacrificing any flavor— and Bobby Ryan, E-276, loves it.**

SERVES **4**   PREPARATION TIME **10 minutes**   COOKING TIME **45 minutes**

### FOR THE MUSHROOM GRAVY

¼ cup (½ stick) butter

3 cloves garlic, minced

10 ounces white mushrooms, sliced

¼ cup flour

3 cups Depression Chicken Stock (page 31) or 1½ (15-ounce) cans reduced-sodium chicken broth

Kosher salt and freshly ground black pepper, to taste

### FOR THE CHICKEN

2 pounds chicken cutlets, rinsed, dried with paper towels, trimmed, halved crosswise, and pounded

Salt and freshly ground black pepper, to taste

1 cup flour

¼ cup olive oil

### TO FINISH THE SANDWICHES

1 loaf Italian bread, split lengthwise, then cut in half crosswise

8 thin slices good-quality deli ham

8 slices Swiss cheese

TO MAKE THE GRAVY: Melt the butter in a medium saucepan over medium-high heat. Add the garlic and sauté for 2 to 3 minutes, until lightly golden. Add the mushrooms, reduce the heat to medium, and sauté another 10 minutes, until most of the moisture from the mushrooms has evaporated. Add the flour and cook another 5 to 6 minutes. Add the chicken stock, stir, and bring to a boil. Reduce the heat and simmer the gravy approximately 15 minutes. Season with salt and pepper to taste.

**WHILE THE GRAVY IS COOKING, MAKE THE CORDON BLEU:** Preheat the oven to 400 degrees. Season the chicken with salt and pepper and dredge it in the flour. Heat the olive oil in a large skillet, preferably cast iron, over medium-high heat. When it's hot enough that a pinch of flour sizzles when dropped into the oil, fry the chicken breasts, in batches if necessary, for 2 to 3 minutes on each side, until golden brown. Check the oil to see if it's hot enough by adding a pinch of flour to the oil to see if it sizzles. Transfer the cutlets to a baking pan as they're done.

**TO FINISH THE SANDWICHES:** Reheat the chicken in the preheated oven for 5 minutes. Place 2 cutlets on each of the 4 pieces of bread. Cover with 2 slices of ham and 2 slices of cheese. Set the open-face sandwiches on a sheet pan and warm in the preheated oven for 7 to 8 minutes, until the cheese melts. Serve immediately with the mushroom gravy ladled over the top.

Lunch Stuff

# Po Boy Chicken Sandwiches

I made these at the firehouse for lunch one day because Jimmy McBrien, L-156, wanted to eat quickly so he could get some things done around the firehouse. Unfortunately for Jimmy, we were very busy that day and didn't sit down to eat lunch until 4 P.M.

You have to get your cast-iron skillet very hot to make this recipe properly. Cooking the sandwiches on a nice hot grill also works well.

SERVES 6    PREPARATION TIME 15 minutes    COOKING TIME 15 minutes

### FOR THE PO BOY SAUCE

1 cup mayonnaise

1 to 2 tablespoons Tabasco sauce

Goya Adobo seasoning or salt and freshly ground black pepper, to taste

¼ cup chopped fresh parsley or cilantro

### FOR THE CHICKEN

½ cup olive oil

2 teaspoons chili powder

1 teaspoon Goya Adobo seasoning

1 teaspoon dried oregano

1 teaspoon cumin

1 teaspoon cayenne pepper (or more, if you like things hot)

1 teaspoon paprika

2½ pounds chicken cutlets, rinsed, trimmed, sliced in half crosswise, and pounded

### FOR THE SANDWICHES

6 fresh rolls

1 head lettuce of your choice, washed and dried

2 ripe tomatoes, sliced

1 red onion, sliced

1.    Preheat the oven to 350 degrees.

**FOR THE SAUCE:** Combine all the sauce ingredients in a mixing bowl and set aside.

**TO COOK THE CHICKEN:** Combine the olive oil, chili powder, Goya Adobo seasoning, oregano, cumin, cayenne pepper, and paprika in a large mixing bowl. Add the chicken cutlets and turn to be sure they are evenly covered with the seasonings. Place a large cast-iron skillet over high heat. When the skillet is hot, add the cutlets, in batches if necessary, and cook until they are dark brown on both sides, 2 to 3 minutes per side. Do not overcrowd the pan, or the meat won't sear and brown properly. Set the cutlets aside as they're done.

**TO ASSEMBLE THE SANDWICHES:** Warm the rolls in the preheated oven. Split them horizontally and spread the bottom half of each roll with the sauce. Add lettuce, tomato, and onion, top with the cutlets, cover with the tops of the rolls, and serve.

Lunch Stuff

# Egg Sandwiches with Peppers, Onions, and Potatoes

**The guys at my firehouse love these sandwiches. I know the number of eggs might seem a bit excessive, but that's how many I use at the firehouse. Besides, if I don't, Frank Malone, E-276, leaves the table hungry.**

SERVES 6    PREPARATION TIME 20 minutes    COOKING TIME 35 to 40 minutes

5 pounds Idaho potatoes

8 cups vegetable oil

½ cup olive oil, or more as needed

Kosher salt and freshly ground black pepper, to taste

3 large onions, peeled and sliced

2 green bell peppers, cored and sliced

2 red bell peppers, cored and sliced

2½ dozen eggs

½ cup fresh chopped basil or parsley

3 loaves Italian bread sliced in half lengthwise and then crosswise

1. Peel the potatoes, cut them in half lengthwise, then slice them ½ inch thick. Place the potatoes in a bowl of cold water as they're sliced so they don't turn brown, but make sure you drain and dry them in batches before putting them in the hot oil to prevent spattering.

2. Turn the oven to warm. Heat the vegetable oil in a deep saucepan over medium-high heat. When the oil reaches 360 degrees on a deep-fat thermometer or when it's hot enough to make a bit of flour sizzle, fry the potatoes in batches to a light golden brown, about 3 to 5 minutes per batch. Transfer them to a baking pan as they're done and season them with kosher salt and pepper. When all the potatoes have been fried, place in the warm oven. Divide the ½ cup olive oil between 2 large skillets over medium-high heat. Sauté the onions and red and green bell peppers in the hot oil for approximately 15 to 20 minutes, until the onions reduce by half. Remove the vegetables from the skillets and set them aside covered. Beat all the eggs, season with salt and pepper, and basil or parsley, and scramble them in the same pans the onions and peppers were cooked in, adding a little more olive oil if necessary, until they are almost done. They should be slightly moist because they will

**Brian DiFusco and Frank Malone showing no fear at a Five Alarm in Brooklyn**

keep cooking. Combine the eggs, potatoes, onions, and peppers, and mix gently. Pile the mixture on half the bread slices, cover with the remaining bread, and serve the sandwiches immediately.

# On-the-Job Training

There are a lot of things probies have to learn on the job—cooking is one of them. A friend of mine told me about the day the guys at his house were making chef salads for lunch. There were two probies on duty. They asked one of them to peel and slice the onions and the other to hard-boil the eggs. Seem simple enough? The men watched in amazement as the first probie picked up an onion and attempted to peel it with a vegetable peeler. Then, about half an hour later, they asked the second probie where the eggs were. He pointed to a pot on the stove. One of the guys lifted the lid to discover a pot full of egg drop soup. Apparently the probie thought you were supposed to crack the eggs before boiling them.

JOHN MISCANIC E-276

Confusion in the kitchen—the boys are putting together a meal

# French Dip Sandwiches

**I love these sandwiches. The first time I tasted one was in Lake Tahoe, where I was working as a cook at Harrah's Hotel and Casino. They served them in the employee cafeteria, and I was hooked. Now the guys at the firehouse are, too.**

SERVES 6    PREPARATION TIME **10 minutes**    COOKING TIME **Approximately 1½ hours**

**1 (5- to 6-pound) eye round roast of beef, rinsed and dried with paper towels**

**3 (15½-ounce) cans beef broth**

**Kosher salt and freshly ground black pepper, to taste**

**3 French baguettes or loaves of Italian bread, sliced open lengthwise and cut in half crosswise**

Follow the directions for cooking the Eye Round Roast au Jus (page 88). When the meat is cooked, set it aside to rest for 15 minutes before slicing. Add 1 can beef broth to the roasting pan and scrape the drippings clinging to the bottom. Transfer the drippings and vegetables from the roasting pan to a saucepan and add the remaining 2 cans of beef broth. Bring the gravy to a slow simmer and simmer for approximately 10 to 15 minutes. Taste and season the gravy with salt and pepper if necessary. Strain the gravy into another pot and set it over low heat to keep warm. Slice the meat as thin as possible and add it to the gravy pot to warm it. Pile the meat on half the bread slices, cover with the remaining bread, and serve with the gravy in a separate bowl. Dip the sandwich in the gravy before every bite. It's delicious!

**VARIATION  You can save time by starting this recipe with 3 pounds cooked sliced roast beef from a delicatessen, but you'll still have to make the gravy. Sauté 2 chopped carrots, 2 stalks celery chopped, and ½ onion chopped in ¼ cup olive oil until soft, about 5 minutes. Add 3 cans beef broth and 3 whole cloves garlic. Bring to a boil, reduce the heat, and simmer for 10 to 15 minutes. Strain, season with salt and pepper to taste, and serve as above.**

Lunch Stuff

# Pulled Pork Sandwich with a Jack and Coke BBQ Sauce

This recipe was a big hit the first time I served it to my extended family. While I was creating the barbecue sauce with the help of my wife, Beth, I was thinking about my good friend and old roommate, Crandall, and how much he would have enjoyed finishing off the Jack and Coke that was leftover from the making of the recipe. He hates to see things go to waste. Here's to you.

SERVES 6    PREPARATION TIME 20 minutes    MARINATING TIME 24 hours
COOKING TIME 3 hours

5 to 6 pounds boneless center cut pork loin or pork shoulder (remove the fat back from the shoulder), sliced in half at its widest point (This could also be made with brisket of beef.)

FOR THE MARINADE

4 cups cola, Dr Pepper, black cherry soda, or root beer

1 cup Worcestershire sauce

2 tablespoons cider vinegar

12 cloves garlic, chopped

1 tablespoon Tabasco sauce

2 teaspoons celery salt

FOR THE JACK AND COKE BBQ SAUCE

1 cup ketchup

⅔ cup cola

⅓ cup Jack Daniel's whiskey

¼ cup Frank's Hot Sauce, or other hot sauce of your choice

2 tablespoons honey

1 tablespoon soy sauce

Goya Adobo seasoning or kosher salt, to taste

6 kaiser rolls

1. Combine the ingredients for the marinade in a bowl, pan, or pot large enough to hold all the pork. Add the pork, turning to be sure it is well coated, cover, and marinate in the refrigerator for 24 hours.

2. Preheat the oven to 350 degrees.

3. Combine the ingredients for the Jack and Coke BBQ Sauce.

4. Place the marinated meat in a roasting pan. Cover the roasting pan with aluminum foil and cook the pork in the preheated oven for 1½ hours. Pour off ⅔ of the liquid in the pan and spread the meat with the barbecue sauce and return it to the oven, uncovered, for another 1½ hours. When the pork is done, it will shred easily with a fork. Test it, and if it's still a bit difficult to shred, return it to the oven for another 15 minutes and try again.

5. When the meat is done, remove it from the oven and shred it with a fork. Slice the rolls in half, pile on the pork, and serve with Creamy Coleslaw (page 157).

That's me in the middle, cooking with Vinny Mattone (left) and John Reynolds, E-317

JERRY RUOTOLO

# Vinny's Hot Beef

**The guys from Engine 319 in Middle Village, Queens, used to tell me about Vinny Mattone's Hot Beef all the time.**

**This dish is simple and spicy. Some of the guys at the firehouse made it to take to the parties they were going to around the holidays. Vinny's family puts it on rice, in a sandwich, on fried eggplant, or eat it as is. He says they serve it at every family get-together. Just make sure you have a nice cold glass of water nearby.**

SERVES **4 to 5**    PREPARATION TIME **15 minutes**    COOKING TIME **20 to 25 minutes**

½ **cup olive oil**

3 **cloves garlic, minced**

1 **pound long Italian hot peppers (green and red), washed and cut into rings**

2 **pounds lean top round beef, all fat removed, sliced thin**

¼ **cup teriyaki sauce**

2 **tablespoons soy sauce**

2 **tablespoons chopped fresh parsley**

In a large skillet, preferably cast iron, heat the oil over medium-high heat. Add the garlic and peppers and cook them down for about 5 to 6 minutes, stirring gently. Add the beef and cook covered for about 5 minutes. Uncover the pan, add the teriyaki sauce and soy sauce, and let the juices reduce by about half, about 2 to 3 minutes. Just before serving, add the parsley and mix gently.

# Steak Salad

This recipe is for flank steak, but you can also use **New York** cut shell steaks, sirloin, or my own favorite, filet mignon. If you use shell steaks or filet mignon, you won't have to marinate them—just oil, season, and pan-sear them.

Whenever I add red meat to a salad, I like to use sweet potatoes. They add color and sweet flavor, they're healthy, and they mix well with almost any kind of salad dressing.

SERVES 6   PREPARATION TIME 15 minutes   COOKING TIME 5 to 10 minutes

**FOR THE MARINADE**

1 cup teriyaki sauce

1 cup soy sauce

½ cup peeled and chopped fresh ginger

12 cloves garlic, peeled and chopped

½ cup sesame oil or vegetable oil


1 (4-pound) flank steak

1 head romaine lettuce, washed, dried, and chopped

1 head red leaf lettuce, washed, dried, and chopped

3 cooked sweet potatoes, peeled and sliced

1 red onion, thinly sliced

12 sliced radishes

Salad dressing of your choice


1. Combine the ingredients for the marinade, add the steak, turning to coat it on all sides, and marinate for at least 2 hours.

2. Preheat the grill to about 500 degrees.

3. Sear the marinated steak on the hot grill for 2 to 3 minutes on each side, then remove it from the grill, cover it, and set it aside for a few minutes while you prepare the salad. Line a large dinner plate with the romaine and red leaf lettuces. Arrange the sliced sweet potatoes over the lettuce. Lower the heat on the grill and finish cooking the steak to desired doneness. Slice the steak thin, against the grain, and arrange the slices over the potatoes. Then garnish with the red onion and radish slices. At the firehouse I serve this with a

dressing made of ⅓ cup balsamic vinegar, ¼ cup water, ½ cup extra virgin olive oil, 1 tablespoon sugar, and 2 teaspoons Goya Adobo seasoning blended for 1 minute until emulsified, but you can use whatever you prefer.

VARIATION **The sweet potatoes can also be cooked on the grill. Slice them about ½ inch thick, brush them with oil, season with salt and pepper, and put them on a medium-hot grill for 3 to 4 minutes on a side, until cooked through.**

MICHAEL SALICA E-276

The boys enjoying the 2001 probie one-year anniversary meal on the apparatus floor. We made Pan-Seared Filet Mignon and steamed lobster with garlic butter

# Meats, Chicken, and Fish

All these main courses are hearty, homey, and delicious. Some, like the brisket, short ribs, and pork shoulder, are slow cooked until they're meltingly tender; others, like the fish and chips and the chicken Francese, are quick and crispy, but all of them are full of flavor and easy to make for a crowd—which is what I serve every night I'm cooking at the firehouse.

# Braised Beef Shanks

When I make a stew, I prefer to cook the meat on the bone to achieve the fullest flavor. Beef shanks also have a considerable amount of marrow, which is what makes the gravy in the stew so velvety and rich. This recipe is a true winter crowd-pleaser. You've really got to try it.

When I make this at the firehouse, I season and sear the beef the night before and store it covered, in the refrigerator. Then all I have to do the next day is slice, dice, and chop the vegetables, and I'm ready to go.

**SERVES** 5 to 6    **PREPARATION TIME** 30 minutes    **COOKING TIME** 3 to 4 hours

4½ to 5 pounds beef shanks

Salt and pepper, to taste

4 tablespoons extra-virgin olive oil

1 large onion, diced

3 cloves garlic, roughly chopped

10 to 12 ounces white mushrooms, quartered

3 carrots, peeled and sliced on the bias into 1-inch pieces

2 stalks celery, sliced on the bias into 1-inch pieces

¼ cup flour

1 cup dry red wine

4 cups beef broth, homemade or canned

1 bay leaf

9 sprigs fresh thyme, or 1 teaspoon dried

1 pound egg noodles, cooked and drained

1.  Season the beef shanks generously with salt and pepper. Heat 2 tablespoons olive oil in a large, heavy pot or Dutch oven over medium-high heat. Brown the shanks in the oil about 4 minutes on each side. Remove them from the pot and set aside.

2.  Add the remaining 2 tablespoons oil to the pot and sauté the onion and garlic over medium-high heat for about 5 minutes, until the onion is translucent. Add the mushrooms and cook 10 minutes, until they release their liquid. Add the carrots and celery and sauté another 5 minutes. Next add the flour, stirring frequently to combine it with the vegeta-

bles and prevent it from sticking, and cook 2 minutes more. Add the wine and reduce for 1 minute, scraping up the browned bits from the bottom of the pan with a wooden spoon. Add the beef broth, bay leaf, and thyme, and return the beef shanks to the pan, making sure they are completely covered by the broth. Add more broth or water if necessary to do this. Bring the stew to a low simmer and cook uncovered for about 3 hours, until the meat falls from the bone. Skim the fat from the top and serve the stew over egg noodles.

**VARIATION** **Instead of the noodles, add ¾ cup barley to the stew for the last half-hour of cooking. This will give you a stew similar to mushroom barley soup, but taken to the next level.**

# Braised Brisket of Beef with Gravy

Because this meat shrinks considerably, we usually purchase a pound or more per man at the firehouse. I also buy extra when I'm feeding my family of four because I love to use the leftovers in sandwiches the next day.

I learned how to cook brisket and corned beef back in the early 1980s when I was working at a Jewish deli and restaurant. My teacher was a large black man named John Henry, who was head cook at the restaurant. He was a good guy and a great teacher, and we always had a lot of fun working together.

Brisket of beef is a rather tough cut of meat, but it can be tender and delicious if properly prepared. This recipe is very basic, and there are lots of things you can do to change its flavors. You can, for example, add teriyaki, garlic, and ginger to the braising liquid for an Asian-accented dish. Or add ketchup, Worcestershire sauce, and chili powder for a spicier gravy.

This is how John Henry taught me to cook a brisket.

SERVES 6 to 7    PREPARATION TIME 5 minutes    COOKING TIME 4 to 4½ hours

1 (7-pound) brisket of beef

Salt, pepper, and garlic powder

**FOR THE GRAVY**

Leftover braising liquid from the roasting pan

½ cup cornstarch

½ cup water

Salt and pepper, to taste

1. Preheat the oven to 500 degrees.

2. Rinse the brisket under cold water. Rub both sides liberally with salt, pepper, and garlic powder to coat the meat completely. Transfer the brisket, fat side up, to a large roasting pan and cook in the preheated oven for 30 minutes, until it is lightly browned. Remove the pan from the oven and cover the meat halfway with cold water. Return the pan to the oven, lower the heat to 350 degrees, and cook for 3½ to 4 hours. It's done when a fork pulls out quickly and easily from the thickest part of the meat. If the fork sticks, cook for another 15 minutes and repeat the test. When the meat is done, transfer it from the pan to a cutting board. Let it rest for 15 minutes before slicing. Meanwhile, pour the liquid

from the pan into a saucepan and bring it to a slow boil, skimming as much fat as possible from the surface. Stir the cornstarch into the water and, when the braising liquid comes to a boil, add the cornstarch mixture, stirring to be sure there are no lumps. When the gravy comes back to a boil, lower the heat and check the consistency of the sauce. If you want it thicker, bring the sauce back to a boil and add more cornstarch and water mixture until you are happy with the consistency. Make sure you bring the sauce back to a boil before adding any more cornstarch mixture, because the cornstarch will not activate unless the sauce is boiling. Taste, and season with salt and pepper.

3.   Brisket can be served with egg noodles or mashed potatoes and a vegetable. It can also be served as an open-face sandwich with the gravy poured on top, or as a nice hot sandwich with the gravy on the side. This dish can also be served like a stew or pot roast, with the vegetables you desire added to the pan for the last hour of cooking. However you serve it, slice the meat thin, against the grain.

# Grandma's Quick and Easy
# Pot Roast

**This recipe was given to me by my mother-in-law. Actually, I hounded her for it, because I think it's a real winner.**

**There are quite a few things I like about it: It's delicious, quick to prepare, healthy, and makes the best leftover sandwiches the following day. And last, but certainly not least, it's inexpensive—which is good at the firehouse.**

SERVES 5 to 6    PREPARATION TIME **10 minutes**    COOKING TIME **2 to 2½ hours**

1 (5-pound) bottom round or rump roast of beef

1 (12-ounce) can beer

3 medium onions, peeled and sliced

6 cloves garlic, peeled and halved

3 (8-ounce) cans tomato sauce

3 (8-ounce) cups water

1 envelope onion soup mix

6 carrots, peeled and chopped into ½-inch pieces

1 (10-ounce) package frozen sweet peas, thawed

3 to 4 tablespoons cornstarch, depending upon how thick you like the sauce

3 to 4 tablespoons cold water

1 tablespoon kosher salt

1 teaspoon pepper

You don't have to season and sear the meat for this recipe, which is what makes its preparation so fast. Rinse the meat under cold water, pat it dry with paper towels, and place it, fat side down, in a large heavy pot or Dutch oven. Add the beer, onions, and garlic to the pot, and pour the tomato sauce directly over the meat. Pour the water around the meat, which should be about ⅔ covered by the liquid. Pour the onion soup mix directly on top of the tomato sauce. Bring the liquid to a boil over medium-high heat, then lower the heat, cover the pot, and simmer the pot roast for about 2 to 2½ hours. At the end of that time, add the carrots and cook for about 15 minutes, then add the peas. After the peas have cooked for 1 or 2 minutes remove the meat to a cutting board. In a small bowl, combine

3 tablespoons cornstarch with 3 tablespoons water and add the mixture to the sauce. Raise the heat so the liquid comes to a quick boil so the cornstarch will thicken it. Reduce the heat again and check the consistency of the sauce. If it's not thick enough, add 1 more tablespoon cornstarch and water and repeat the process. Add the salt and pepper and remove the sauce from the heat. Trim any remaining fat from the meat, and slice it as thin as possible against the grain.

My mother-in-law serves it over egg noodles with a healthy ladle of the sauce. Try it . . . you'll like it.

## The Tale of the Disappearing Pot Roast

**"Señor man," Papi Rivas, was in the middle of cooking a 12-pound pot roast at his fire station, Engine-50, Ladder-19, in the South Bronx, when the alarm went off. Before everyone took off, one of his buddies shouted to him to turn down the oven. "No problem, I've got it covered," he shouted back, in a thick Latino accent. But when they all returned an hour and a half later, and much hungrier than when they'd left, there was nothing in the pot but a muddy brown soup. Everything—meat, potatoes, onion, carrots, and parsley—had completely liquefied. It seemed that in his haste to put out the fire they'd been called to, Papi had turned the heat in the oven *up* instead of down. You can bet he heard about that for a long time to come—and still does.**

# Short Ribs of Beef
# with Pepperoncini

The addition of pepperoncini and mushrooms gives these braised short ribs a unique pungency that, combined with the deep flavor of the beef and the earthy vegetables, makes this dish a complex culinary delight.

SERVES **4 to 5**   PREPARATION TIME **45 minutes**   COOKING TIME **3 to 4 hours**

**4 pounds beef short ribs**

**Salt and freshly ground pepper, to taste**

**Flour for dredging**

**2 to 3 tablespoons olive oil**

**1 medium onion, diced**

**2 carrots, peeled and cut into 1-inch chunks**

**2 stalks celery, cut into 1-inch chunks**

**10 ounces white mushrooms, quartered**

**3 cloves garlic, peeled**

**1 cup dry red wine**

**4 cups Beef Stock (page 30) or 2 (15½-ounce) cans beef broth**

**½ cup pepperoncini juice, reserved from the jar**

**8 sprigs fresh thyme**

**½ cup dried white beans soaked overnight and drained, or 1 (15½-ounce) can white beans with their liquid**

**9 whole pepperoncini peppers**

Season the short ribs with salt and pepper and dredge them in flour to coat all sides. In a large pot or Dutch oven, heat the olive oil over a medium-high heat. When the oil is hot, add the ribs in batches and brown them lightly on all sides. Remove them from the pan and set them aside as they're done. When all the ribs are browned, add the onion, carrots, celery, mushrooms, and garlic to the pot and cook for about 15 minutes, until all the vegetables soften. Dust the vegetables with ¼ cup flour, stirring constantly, and cook another minute. Add the red wine and scrape up any browned bits sticking to the bottom of the pan. Cook, stirring, until the liquid thickens, about 30 seconds. Add the beef stock, pepperoncini juice, thyme, beans, and the browned ribs, and bring the mixture to a simmer. Turn down the heat and simmer very slowly for approximately 3 to 3½ hours. Remove the ribs from the pot and skim as much fat as possible from the surface of the stew. Return the ribs to the pot, add the pepperoncini peppers, and simmer another half-hour. I like to serve this over spaghetti squash, but it's equally good all on its own.

# Eye Round Roast au Jus

**What could be more satisfying than a nice hot roast on a cold winter night? Serve this with baked sweet potatoes and string beans, and you've got a great meal. What I really like about an eye round is that it's not expensive, it isn't very fatty, it has great flavor, and it's very tender.**

SERVES 6 to 7  PREPARATION TIME 10 minutes

COOKING TIME approximately 1½ hours

> 1 (5- to 6-pound) eye round of beef, rinsed and dried with paper towels
>
> ¼ cup extra-virgin olive oil
>
> Salt and freshly ground black pepper, to taste
>
> 2 carrots, roughly chopped
>
> 2 stalks celery, roughly chopped
>
> ½ medium onion, chopped
>
> 3 cloves garlic, unpeeled
>
> 2½ cups cold water

1.  Preheat the oven to 350 degrees.

2.  Place the eye round in a roasting pan, rub with the olive oil, and season liberally on all sides with salt and pepper. Add the carrots, celery, onion, garlic, and 1 cup cold water to the pan and roast in the preheated oven for approximately 1½ to 1¾ hours. Check the meat with a meat thermometer after 1 hour, 15 minutes—it should be 125 to 130 degrees for rare to medium. If you don't have a meat thermometer, insert a roasting fork into the thickest part of the meat. Remove the fork and touch it to your lips. If it's cold to warm, cook the roast another 15 minutes and check again. If the fork is very warm to hot, your roast is done medium-well.*

3.  Transfer the roast to a cutting board and let sit 15 minutes before carving. Meanwhile, add 1½ cups cold water to the roasting pan and scrape up all the browned bits clinging to the bottom with a wooden spoon. Transfer the contents of the pan to a medium saucepan and

*I like my roast medium-rare, and, in any case, you can always put a piece back for those who like their meat cooked longer. Another trick is to cut the meat in half crosswise so there will be four end pieces rather than just two, for people who like well-done meat.

simmer about 15 minutes. Strain the vegetables from the liquid and season the "jus" with salt and pepper. Slice the meat as thinly as possible with a sharp knife. Serve immediately with a little of the pan juices poured over the top.

## Anniversary, Promotion, or Retirement Meals

**The nicest and most expensive meals at the firehouse are usually those that are served to celebrate a firefighter's anniversary, promotion, or retirement.**

**If it's a firefighter's anniversary, he generally buys and makes a nice meal for the brothers, and no one has to pitch in any money.**

**If it's a promotion or retirement meal, a list goes up in the firehouse to find out how many guys are going to be able to attend, and the person who's being promoted or is retiring buys the provisions. A typical meal might be a surf-and-turf with a baked potato and a vegetable. Again, none of the men has to put up any money. This always makes the guys very happy.**

MICHAEL SALICA E-276

George Murphy, E-276, playing the bagpipes at our party for retiring Chief Norman Whalen, Bn-33

# Pan-Seared Filet Mignon

**The guys at the firehouse request this dish for their anniversary meal or when they are coming off probation. Filet mignon is excellent with shrimp scampi or lobster as the turf part of a "surf-and-turf" dinner. You can cut the steaks from a whole fillet yourself, or ask the butcher to do it for you.**

SERVES **6 to 7**   PREPARATION TIME **15 minutes**   COOKING TIME **15 to 20 minutes**

**1 whole 6- to 7-pound fillet of beef, trimmed and cut into 12 to 14 (4- to 5-ounce) steaks**

**Olive oil, to lightly cover the fillets**

**Kosher salt and pepper, to taste**

1. Preheat the oven to 350 degrees.

2. Lay the fillets out on a sheet pan, brush both sides lightly with olive oil, and season with salt and pepper.

3. Place a large skillet, preferably cast iron, over medium-high heat and wait until it is hot but not smoking. Place the fillets in the hot pan in batches of 4 or 5 and sear them for 2 to 3 minutes on each side, until they are evenly browned. Set them aside on a sheet pan as they're done. When all the fillets have been seared, put them in the preheated oven for approximately 5 to 7 minutes, until they are medium rare. Serve immediately.

4. If some of the guys like them a little more done, leave them in an extra 1 or 2 minutes. I hate to see such an expensive and tender cut of meat cooked anything past medium; to me it's such a waste.

# Steak au Poivre with a Mushroom Green Peppercorn Dijon Sauce

This is the main dish my friend Dave and I made for our "food fight" with the New York City cops on The Food Network. When we found out that our main ingredient was going to be New York cut shell steaks, I was delighted! The sauce had to be made without any alcohol, so I boosted this one with a blend of textures and flavors.

SERVES 2    PREPARATION TIME 15 minutes    COOKING TIME 15 to 20 minutes

**FOR THE STEAK**

2 (12- to 16-ounce) boneless New York cut shell steaks (if the steaks are thick, pound them lightly.)

2 tablespoons Dijon mustard, or more, to taste

Kosher salt, to taste

2 tablespoons coarsely ground black pepper (enough to cover both sides of the steaks)

2 tablespoons olive oil

**FOR THE SAUCE**

4 tablespoons (½ stick) butter

2 cloves garlic, minced

¼ cup minced shallots

8 ounces white mushrooms, sliced

1 cup beef broth

½ cup whipping cream

1 tablespoon Dijon mustard

2 tablespoons green peppercorns packed in brine

Salt, to taste

TO MAKE THE STEAKS: Spread both sides of each steak with a thin coating of mustard. Sprinkle with salt and cover both sides with pepper. Heat the olive oil in a large, heavy skillet over medium-high heat and cook the steaks 3 to 4 minutes on each side. They should be rare at this point. Set them aside lightly covered to stay warm. Do not wash the pan.

**TO MAKE THE SAUCE:** Heat the butter in a sauté pan over medium-high heat and sauté the garlic and shallots for about 1 minute. Add the mushrooms, raise the heat to high, and cook for about 5 minutes. Then add the broth, cream, mustard, peppercorns, and salt and reduce the sauce by half.

**TO ASSEMBLE AND SERVE:** Reheat the skillet in which you cooked the steaks over medium-high heat. Add the steaks and cook for another 2 minutes on each side for medium-rare. Transfer them to dinner plates and top with a nice coating of sauce. You should have some sauce left over to pass on the side.

Hamming it up for the camera before "Food Fight"

# Barbecued Pork Ribs

These ribs are as good as any I have ever eaten. They're juicy, tender, and finger-lickin' good. Needless to say, they're always a big hit at the firehouse. I use the pork loin back ribs (these are the ribs they remove from a loin of pork to make it boneless). You could also use baby back ribs, which are essentially the same but taken when the pig is smaller. Baby backs are the most tender ribs.

SERVES 6 (½ rack per person, the perfect amount to go with BBQ chicken)

PREPARATION TIME 10 minutes   COOKING TIME 1½ hours   GRILLING TIME 5 minutes

**6 pounds pork loin back ribs (3 [2-pound] racks) or baby back ribs**

**DRY RUB**

**3 teaspoons Goya Adobo seasoning**

**2 teaspoons brown sugar**

**½ teaspoon cayenne pepper**

**½ teaspoon chili powder**

**½ teaspoon allspice**

**JACK AND COKE BBQ SAUCE**

**I cup ketchup**

**⅔ cup cola**

**⅓ cup Jack Daniel's whiskey**

**¼ cup Frank's Hot Sauce, or the hot sauce of your choice**

**2 tablespoons honey**

**I tablespoon soy sauce**

**Goya Adobo seasoning or kosher salt, to taste**

1. Preheat the oven to 350 degrees.

2. Leave the racks whole or cut them in half to fit them in your baking pan.

3. Combine the ingredients for the dry rub and cover the ribs completely with the mixture. Place the ribs in a roasting pan meat side up, covering the bottom of the pan with about ⅓ inch water. Cover the pan with aluminum foil and cook the ribs in the preheated oven for 45 minutes.

4. Thoroughly combine the ingredients for the BBQ sauce. Remove the pan from the oven, brush the tops of the ribs with the sauce, and return them to the oven uncovered for 45 minutes. If you're using a charcoal grill, get the fire going. If you're using a gas grill, turn it to medium-high to preheat during the last 5 minutes or so of the ribs' cooking time. Remove the ribs from the oven and coat the top side of the racks with BBQ sauce. Place the ribs on the grill top side down and cook 1 to 2 minutes, until you can see grill marks. Sauce the underside of the racks, turn them over, and cook another 2 minutes. Reapply BBQ sauce to the top side, flip again, and cook another 2 minutes. Reapply sauce to the underside and flip again. Remove the racks from the grill, place them on a cutting board, and slice between the ribs one by one. Serve immediately with lots of paper napkins.

# Parmesan-Crusted Pork Chops

**My friend Timmy Brannigan, the chef, gave me this recipe. He said the customers at his restaurant love it and that it would be a great dish to serve at the firehouse because it's so easy to make. He was right!**

SERVES 4    PREPARATION TIME 5 minutes    COOKING TIME 20 minutes

8 (1-inch-thick) center cut pork chops on the bone or boneless pork loin

Salt and freshly ground black pepper, to taste

2 tablespoons extra-virgin olive oil

Dijon mustard, to coat chops

1 cup freshly grated Parmesan or Romano cheese

1. Preheat the oven to 350 degrees.

2. Season the chops on both sides with salt and pepper. Heat the olive oil in a heavy skillet. When the oil is hot enough to make a drop of water sizzle, add the chops and sear them for about 3 minutes on each side. When they are lightly browned, remove them from the pan. Coat the tops with the mustard and then the grated cheese, transfer the chops to a sheet pan, and finish cooking them in the preheated oven for approximately 10 to 12 minutes. I like to serve these with braised red cabbage and Classic Mashed Potatoes (page 155).

# Pernil (Marinated Roasted Pork Shoulder)

My friend Kris Andreassen's wife, Milena Cepeda, and her whole family cook delicious Dominican food. I kept nagging Milena to ask her mother how she makes this recipe and another great dish, Gandules and Rice (page 141), and, after about a month of my persistence, she and her mom were nice enough to give me the recipes and show me how to make them. I would like to take this opportunity to thank them both and to pass their great recipes on to you.

This one is savory, melt-in-your-mouth scrumptious. You'll want to bottle the glorious aromas that will fill your home when you cook it. You can marinate it for as short a time as 15 minutes, which is how I do it at the firehouse, but Milena says it's best if you marinate it in the refrigerator overnight. If you love fresh ham, you will love this.

SERVES 4    PREPARATION TIME 20 minutes    COOKING TIME 3 hours

¾ teaspoon dried oregano

2 tablespoons Goya Adobo seasoning

6 to 9 cloves garlic, to taste

1 packet Goya Sazon with achiote and cilantro

½ cup distilled white vinegar

1 (7-pound) pork shoulder or fresh ham

1.  Preheat oven to 325 degrees.

2.  Place the oregano, Goya Adobo seasoning, garlic, and Goya Sazon in a food processor and pulse a few times to combine them and chop the garlic. Add 2 tablespoons vinegar and pulse again until the mixture becomes a fine paste. Add the remaining vinegar and pulse once more. Take a small whiff of the marinade and your mouth should start to water.

3.  Rinse the pork shoulder under cold water, dry it, and lay it on a cutting board. With the tip of a chef's knife, pierce the meat in several places on both sides all the way down to the bone. Turn the knife in a circular motion to create small pockets that will hold the marinade. Transfer the meat to a roasting pan, skin side up, and spoon the marinade into all the pockets to fill them. Cover the roasting pan with aluminum foil and let the pork marinate

for about 15 minutes, or, for an even tastier result, marinate it in the refrigerator overnight. Re-cover the Pernil with the aluminum foil, and roast it in the preheated oven for approximately 3 hours. Test it with a fork. It's done when the meat easily pulls away from the bone. Serve it with Gandules and Rice (page 141) and pan gravy.

# My Meatballs

I suspect that every Italian family on the planet has its own meatball recipe, so this is for all you non-Italians out there. Most Italian mothers and grandmothers fry their meatballs to a crispy perfection. I'm going to show you a way to make them without frying. They taste just as good, but they are quicker and easier to prepare. When Chief Bynum of Bn-33 saw me preparing them one day he told me there were only three or four people whose meatballs he'd eat. Now he eats mine, too.

MAKES 30 to 36 meatballs    PREPARATION TIME 20 minutes    COOKING TIME 15 minutes

I pound ground beef

I pound ground pork

I pound ground veal

2 cups freshly grated Romano cheese

1½ cups plain breadcrumbs

2 eggs, beaten

2 cloves garlic, minced

3 tablespoons chopped fresh parsley

½ teaspoon salt

½ teaspoon freshly ground black pepper

½ cup extra-virgin olive oil, or more as needed

1. Preheat the oven to 400 degrees.

2. In a large mixing bowl, combine all the ingredients except the oil and mix thoroughly with your hands. Roll the mixture into meatballs approximately 1 to 1¼ inches in diameter. You should have a total of 30 to 36. Put ½ cup olive oil in a small bowl, roll the meatballs in the oil to cover each one completely, and set them in a baking dish. Bake in the preheated oven for 15 minutes. That's it! Serve them over spaghetti with My Marinara Sauce or on a roll with tomato sauce and mozzarella cheese for a meatball parmigiana sandwich.

# Is He Kidding?

Our former captain at Ladder-156 George Cassidy was a real joker with a dry sense of humor. One day during lunch Captain was up to his old jokes, carrying on with Jimmy McBrien and Jimmy "Muligooch" Mulligan, L-156, about how dry the meatballs they'd made for lunch were. All of a sudden Captain stopped talking. He started coughing a little bit and was turning red. The guys looked at him, started laughing, and resumed their conversation. They really thought he was kidding. Luckily, Mulligooch realized how dry the meatballs actually were. He jumped up and gave Captain the Heimlich maneuver, dislodging the food from his throat. (By this time, the guys said, Captain was as purple as Barney the dinosaur.) When he could talk again, he said, "Don't ever ask me to eat meatballs when these two Irish guys are making them!" He pushed his plate to the center of the table, and the guys just smiled and divvied up the remaining meatballs.

So remember, it's all fun and games until the captain turns blue!

MICHAEL SALICA E-276

Captain Cassidy (retired) (top middle) trying to teach Bobby Sputh, E-276, to Salsa while Bobby Ryan (bottom right) tries to get his point across

# Chicken Cacciatore

This is always a special request from my captain, Brian Lake. He brings up Chicken Cacciatore every time we talk about food; I'm telling you, he's obsessed. If I'm cooking and he's working, this is what he asks me to make.

SERVES 4 to 5    PREPARATION TIME 30 minutes    COOKING TIME 45 minutes

Flour, to coat chicken before frying

2 (2½- to 3-pound) chickens, cut into 8 pieces with the breasts cut into thirds

¾ cup olive oil

6 cloves garlic, peeled and halved

10 to 12 ounces white mushrooms, sliced

1 large onion, peeled and sliced

2 green bell peppers, cored, seeded, and sliced into ½-inch strips

2 red bell peppers, cored, seeded, and cut into ½-inch strips

1 cup dry white wine

1 (15½-ounce) can chicken broth

1 (28-ounce) can whole tomatoes, with their juice, crushed

1 teaspoon crushed red pepper

Kosher salt, to taste

1 teaspoon dried oregano

2 to 3 tablespoons tomato paste

6 leaves fresh basil, chopped

1. Place the flour in a shallow dish and coat the chicken pieces, shaking off any excess. Heat the oil in a large saucepot over medium-high heat. Add the chicken in batches and fry until golden brown on all sides. When all the chicken has been cooked, set it aside. Add the garlic to the pan and cook until it turns golden brown. Add the mushrooms and sauté for 5 to 7 minutes, until they release most of their liquid. Add the onion and green and red bell peppers and sauté until the vegetables are soft, approximately 6 minutes. Add the wine and let reduce for about a minute. Add the chicken broth, tomatoes, crushed red pepper, salt, oregano, and tomato paste. Return the chicken to the pot and bring the liquid to a

Meats, Chicken, and Fish

boil, stirring constantly. Turn down the heat and simmer for 30 to 45 minutes. Stir in the fresh basil just before serving.

2. This dish goes well with any pasta or rice, and it tastes even better the following day.

## "Gulling"

Sometimes guys are considered "gulls" (meaning seagulls), because, like gulls swooping down to snatch scraps from a fishing boat, they show up around lunchtime at the firehouse on their day off, swoop down for the meal, and never offer to pay. If this happened just once in a while, it would be fine, but true gulls can't help themselves. You'll find them hovering over the table while the rest of the guys are eating just waiting for scraps. Or they'll claim to be out on the meal, then you'll find them raiding the refrigerator later, looking for leftovers. These are the guys firefighters love to mess with.

Leftover chili can always be doctored up with huge quantities of cayenne pepper and salt. Sometimes doughnuts have the "crème" blown out and replaced with a new and improved mayo and mustard filling. At my firehouse, cardboard "chicken cutlets" were once left in the fridge for a certain firefighter who couldn't quite part with his money to pay for the meal. He was caught swooping down and trying to get his dirty little claws in those cutlets while everyone's back was turned.

Firefighters are extremely creative when it comes to getting even with seagulls. "Yeeeep . . . Yeeeeeeep." (That, by the way, is the universal seagull noise heard around the firehouse.)

# Chicken Francese

Whenever I make this at the firehouse, the guys don't seem to say very much, they just eat. That makes me proud. This recipe is pretty simple, it just takes a while to prepare. You've got to be patient and focused while you're frying the chicken breasts. After that, it's all downhill.

SERVES 4 to 5    PREPARATION TIME 45 minutes    COOKING TIME 10 minutes

2 cups flour

6 eggs, beaten

I cup vegetable oil

2½ pounds skinless, boneless chicken breasts, rinsed, trimmed, and pounded

Salt and freshly ground pepper, to taste

FOR THE SAUCE:

I stick (¼ pound) butter

I clove garlic, peeled and minced

I cup white wine

I½ cups chicken broth, canned or homemade

Juice of I to I½ lemons

2 teaspoons kosher salt

¼ cup water

¼ cup cornstarch

2 tablespoons chopped fresh parsley

1. Preheat the oven to 350 degrees.

2. Put the flour in one bowl and the eggs in another. Heat the oil in a large cast-iron skillet over medium heat. While the oil is heating, salt and pepper the chicken breasts, then dip them in the flour and then in the egg. It's important to make sure you completely cover the entire breast in flour and egg before it's placed in the oil. Check the oil by dropping in a pinch of flour. If the oil sizzles, it is hot enough. Do not add the chicken until the oil is hot enough, and don't overcrowd the pan. Cook the chicken in batches, removing it to drain

on paper towels as soon as it's golden brown on both sides. Once the chicken pieces have drained, transfer them to a baking dish and set aside while you prepare the sauce.

TO PREPARE THE SAUCE: Place the butter in a saucepan over medium heat. As it begins to melt, add the garlic. When the butter is completely melted, add the wine, chicken broth, lemon juice, and salt. Taste and, if necessary, correct the seasoning. Raise the heat to medium-high to bring the sauce to a simmer, close to a boil. In a small mixing bowl, combine the water and cornstarch. When the sauce comes to a simmer, add the cornstarch and water mixture and wait until the sauce returns to a simmer to activate the cornstarch, which will thicken it ever so slightly. Add the parsley and stir.

3.   Lightly ladle some of the sauce over the chicken breasts to keep them moist and put them in the preheated oven for 10 minutes. Remove the chicken from the oven and serve immediately with the remaining sauce ladled over it.

# Chicken Marsala

This dish is also up near the top of the list of firehouse favorites. The key to its wonderful flavor is cooking the mushrooms until they've released most of their liquid, shrunk, and turned a dark brown.

SERVES 4 to 6    PREPARATION TIME 20 minutes    COOKING TIME 20 to 30 minutes

¼ cup extra-virgin olive oil, or more, if needed

2 pounds skinless and boneless chicken breasts trimmed, sliced through horizontally, rinsed, and pounded flat

Salt and freshly ground pepper, to taste

1 cup flour, for dredging chicken, plus 3 tablespoons for the mushrooms

¼ cup (½ stick) butter

3 cloves garlic, minced

10 to 12 ounces white mushrooms, sliced

¾ cup Marsala wine

1 (15½-ounce) can low-sodium chicken broth

2 tablespoons chopped fresh parsley, sage, or thyme

Salt and freshly ground black pepper, to taste

Heat ¼ cup oil in a large skillet, preferably cast iron, over medium-high heat. While the oil is heating, season the chicken breasts with salt and pepper and dredge them in 1 cup flour. Check to see if the oil is hot enough by dropping a pinch of flour into the pan; if the oil sizzles, it's hot enough. Cook the chicken breasts in batches for 2 to 3 minutes on each side, adding more oil to the pan if necessary, until they turn golden brown. When all the chicken has browned, set it aside and add the butter to the pan. When the butter has melted, add the garlic and cook until golden brown. Add the mushrooms and cook 10 minutes. Sprinkle them with the remaining 3 tablespoons flour and stir until all the flour has been absorbed. Cook the mushrooms 3 to 5 more minutes. When they have turned dark brown and reduced considerably in size, add the wine, scrape up any bits from the bottom of the pan with a wooden spoon, and let the liquid reduce by half. Add the chicken stock and simmer for another 3 minutes. Add the fresh herbs and salt and pepper to taste. Return the chicken to the sauce in the pan to reheat for approximately 1 minute. Serve at once.

# Garlicky Lemon Chicken

This dish is definitely a firehouse favorite. In fact, FF Jimmy Martinetion of Engine 50 rated it "best firehouse meal." But it's just as good to serve at a party or for your family as it is at the firehouse. It's inexpensive and healthy, the lemon and garlic give it delicious flavor, and the chicken stays nice and moist.

SERVES 6    PREPARATION TIME 15 minutes    COOKING TIME 1 hour

3 whole chickens, split in half, rinsed, and patted dry with paper towels

Salt and freshly ground black pepper, to taste

9 cloves garlic, peeled and minced

Grated zest of 1 lemon (optional)

Freshly squeezed juice of 6 lemons

½ cup olive oil

1 teaspoon crushed red pepper

1 teaspoon dried oregano

⅛ cup chopped fresh parsley

1.  Preheat oven to 400 degrees.

2.  Season the chicken with salt and pepper, arrange it in a roasting pan, and cook in the pre-heated oven for 50 minutes. While the chicken is cooking, combine all the remaining ingredients in a mixing bowl in the order they are listed. The marinade should be tangy, salty, and pleasantly garlicky.

3.  After 50 minutes, the juice of the chicken should run clear when the thigh is pierced with a fork. Remove it from the oven and let it cool for a few minutes. Turn the oven to broil. Separate the thigh and leg portions from the breast and wing portions. Separate the wings

Don't ever try to cut corners by using jarred prepared garlic. Not only does it not taste like garlic, but also it has a metallic sulphur odor that stays on your breath and comes out through your pores far longer than fresh garlic. It takes just a few seconds to peel a clove of garlic. Go for it.

from the breasts, and cut the breasts into thirds. Then separate the legs from the thighs. Return the chicken pieces to the pan, spoon the marinade over all, and broil for 5 to 10 minutes, until the chicken turns a dark golden brown. Transfer it to a serving platter or individual plates, scrape up all the good baked-on flavors from the bottom of the roasting pan, and pour the juices into a gravy boat to ladle over the chicken.

4. I like to serve this with Gandules and Rice (page 141) or just a simple green salad.

# Nicolosi's Hairy Hawaiian Chicken

Generally speaking, I don't really like to mix fruits with meat or poultry, but this dish is an exception. I got the recipe from FF Paul Nicolosi of L-156. It's not difficult, but it does take a while to fry the cubed chicken and then bake in the oven. The result, however, is definitely worth the time. It's not dietetic, but it's definitely comfort food. Don't even bother asking why it's called hairy; let's not go there. I like to add crushed red pepper, too, so the tastes are sweet, sour, and hot.

**SERVES** 8   **PREPARATION TIME** 30 minutes   **COOKING TIME** 1 hour

2 cups flour

4 to 6 eggs, beaten with a little milk

3 to 4 cups plain breadcrumbs

4 pounds skinless and boneless chicken, cut into cubes

Vegetable oil, for frying

1 (40-ounce) jar duck sauce (sweet and sour sauce)

3 (15½-ounce) cans pineapple chunks with their juice

1.  Preheat the oven to 350 degrees.

2.  In three separate shallow dishes, place the flour, eggs, and breadcrumbs. In batches, dredge the cubed chicken in the flour first, then dip it in the egg wash, and finally, dredge it in the breadcrumbs, making sure to cover the cubes thoroughly with each ingredient. Spread the breaded cubes on a clean sheet tray as they're done.

3.  Fill a large heavy skillet halfway with vegetable oil and set it over medium-high heat. When the oil is hot enough to sizzle when you drop in a bit of flour, fry the breaded chicken cubes in batches until they're golden brown. Remove the cooked cubes to a clean sheet tray lined with paper towels. Don't overcrowd the pan or the chicken will steam instead of frying. When all the cubes have been fried, transfer the chicken to a baking dish. In a separate mixing bowl, combine the duck sauce and the pineapple chunks.

4.  Pour the mixture over the chicken and place it in the preheated oven to cook for 45 minutes. Remove from the oven and check to be sure the chicken is piping hot. The boys at the firehouse like me to serve this dish with white rice.

# Breast of Lamb in a Red Sauce

**Breast of lamb is really the underside of the rib cage. The ribs have very little meat on them, but they have loads of flavor, which gives the tomato sauce a velvety delectability. I got this recipe from Geri, who is married to my former roommate, Gardner Crandall. Gardner is now a chef at the Marriot Hotel in Albany, New York. Geri told me that her mom makes it all the time and that it's not only delicious but very easy. I tried it myself, and she's right on both counts. She also told me it was even better the next day, and she's right about that, too.**

SERVES 6 to 8    PREPARATION TIME 20 minutes    COOKING TIME 2 to 3 hours

1 (4- to 5-pound) breast of lamb

Salt and freshly ground black pepper, to taste

1 tablespoon olive oil

½ cup red wine (optional)

1 (4- to 6-ounce) can tomato paste

3 (28-ounce) cans crushed tomatoes

1 (28-ounce) can water

Kosher salt and red crushed pepper, to taste

Rinse the lamb under cold water, dry it with paper towels, and season it liberally with salt and pepper. Heat the oil in a large saucepan over medium-high heat and sear the lamb on both sides until it turns a rich brown, about 5 minutes per side. You can cut the breast in half or in thirds if it's too big to fit into the pan in one piece. Remove the seared lamb and drain the oil from the pan, but don't wash the pan. Return the pan to the heat, add the red wine, and reduce the liquid by about half, scraping up any browned bits that cling to the bottom with a wooden spoon. Stir in the tomato paste and cook for 1 minute. Add the crushed tomatoes and water. Bring the liquid to a simmer, return the lamb to the pan, and simmer the sauce for at least 2, preferably 3 hours, skimming the oil as it rises to the top of the sauce. Season the sauce with kosher salt and crushed red pepper. Remove the lamb from the sauce and slice between the ribs to separate them. Serve the sauce over your favorite pasta with the ribs on top, and enjoy.

VARIATION: **When I make this sauce, I like to sauté 1 diced onion and 3 cloves garlic before adding the red wine and tomato paste, but the choice is yours. It's delicious either way.**

Meats, Chicken, and Fish

# Firehouse Pranks

Firefighting is definitely not for everyone. Being a firefighter is both dangerous and stressful, and that's one of the reasons, I believe, that firefighters laugh so much together, hang out together after work, and pull so many pranks on one another.

Every firehouse has its stories, and I love listening to them all. One of my friends told me this one:

Generally probies don't get to go up to the rack (the bunkroom) to rest until 12 or 1 A.M. when the chores are done. One night at about 3 A.M. my friend and the three other guys on duty decided it was time to "mess with" one of the probies.

They tiptoed into the bunkroom where the probie was sleeping. One of them was armed with an empty water can filled with pressurized air attached to an old air horn from one of the fire trucks. Two others had high-powered flashlights. The fourth guy lifted the end of the bed and slammed it down. As soon as it hit the floor, the probie jumped up. The guys with the flashlights turned them on at the same time their cohort hit the siren. The kid thought he was being run over by a fire truck. My friend said the probie was white as a sheet and it took them a long time to calm him down. He also suggested that if I wanted to try this with the guys at my house we make sure to pick a victim who was under the age of 25 with a good, strong heart.

JOHN MISCANIC E-276

Sean Murray, E-276, getting bucketed. Luckily he's a good swimmer

# Fresh Salmon Cakes

This recipe takes a bit of work, but it is *so* worth it. To make it easier, the cakes can be prepared and cooked in advance, then frozen. Just defrost and reheat them when you're ready to serve. The Ritz crackers give the cakes a richness that I really like. If you don't have Ritz crackers on hand, or if you'd like to reduce the calorie content of the recipe, use plain breadcrumbs and substitute evaporated skim milk for the heavy cream. I like to serve these scrumptious salmon cakes topped with a simple mayo and Tabasco dressing.

I made these cakes at the firehouse when *O: The Oprah Magazine* came to interview me in December 2001, and I wasn't sure how they'd be received because some of the guys just don't like salmon. Well, much to my relief, the guys raved about them, which gave me a real ego-boost. If the guys liked them, I thought, Oprah's readers were going to love them. Firemen don't always tell you what they like about a dish, but they'll almost always tell you what they don't like!

MAKES approximately 16 (4-ounce) cakes    PREPARATION TIME 20 minutes
COOKING TIME 30 minutes

3 pounds skinless salmon fillets, diced into ¼-inch cubes

2 cups crumbled Ritz crackers

½ cup heavy cream

½ red onion, diced

2 cloves garlic, minced

3 tablespoons chopped fresh dill (or parsley or cilantro)

3 tablespoons Dijon mustard

3 eggs

1 teaspoon Tabasco sauce

1 teaspoon kosher salt

1 cup flour

½ to ¾ cup olive oil

2 lemons, each cut into 6 wedges, for garnish

Meats, Chicken, and Fish

1. Preheat the oven to 350 degrees.

2. Place everything except the flour, oil, and lemons in a large mixing bowl and fold together with a spoon or spatula. Gently form the mixture into ¼-pound "burgers." The mixture will be very loose, and that's the way it should be; you just have to handle it carefully so it doesn't fall apart. Place the flour on a dish and flour both sides of the patties. Next, put about 2 tablespoons olive oil in a large cast-iron skillet over medium heat. The oil is hot enough when you add a smidgen of flour and it sizzles on contact. Now add a few salmon cakes to the skillet, cooking them until they're golden brown, about 2 to 3 minutes per side. Continue adding oil as needed and cooking the cakes in batches, setting them aside on a sheet pan as they're done. When you have completed frying the cakes, place the sheet pan in the preheated oven for 5 to 7 minutes until they are warm all the way through. Garnish with the lemon wedges. These can be served on a bun, on a bed of lettuce, or simply on a plate with your favorite side dish.

JERRY RUOTOLO

**Cooking the meal for *O: The Oprah Magazine*. The guys were happy. They got a "free-O" meal of Garlic Ginger Teriyaki Shrimp, Fresh Salmon Cakes, and Gandules and Rice**

# The Joy of Cast-Iron Cooking

For me, there's no better cooking utensil than an old-fashioned cast-iron skillet or pot. In fact, I'm sure that when pots and pans were passed down through the generations, those cast-iron pans caused a fair amount of sibling rivalry. But aside from the fact that the pans look great and make fine family heirlooms, there's a lot more to be said about the joys of cooking in cast iron.

Cast iron is thicker and heavier and, therefore, takes a bit longer to heat than other metals, but it also holds the heat more consistently than any other metal. This means that it won't cool down as much or take as long to reheat as you add ingredients to the pan, and you won't have to keep adjusting the flame to make sure whatever you're cooking doesn't burn.

I'm not sure why, but cast-iron cookware is generally about 25 percent less expensive than most other pans. Perhaps it's because cleaning cast iron is a bit more labor-intensive than cleaning some other surfaces. But once you learn how to handle and season it, I promise you'll never look back.

I season my new pans by oiling them completely, inside and outside. I preheat the oven to 500 degrees and put a piece of foil on the middle rack, then put the pan upside down on the foil and let it "cook" for I hour.

I try not to use soap on a cast-iron pan unless there's just too much burnt-on food to simply wipe it out. But whether or not I've actually washed it, I *always* oil it before putting it away to keep it from rusting. (If you don't use your cast iron often, skip the oiling, because the oil might turn rancid. Just make sure to dry the pan completely before putting it away.)

# Lemony Garlic-Baked Salmon

This particular salmon dish is one of my absolute favorites. When I made it at the fire-house, a lot of the guys wanted the recipe. In fact, FF Kevin Donovan of L-19 told me that he's made it at home several times. As far as compliments go in the firehouse, you don't get much better than that.

SERVES 6   PREPARATION TIME 15 minutes   COOKING TIME 25 minutes

6 (8- to 10-ounce) salmon fillets

Freshly squeezed juice of 3 fresh lemons (about $\frac{1}{2}$ cup juice)

Grated zest of 2 lemons

6 to 9 cloves garlic, finely chopped

$\frac{1}{4}$ cup olive oil

2 teaspoons salt

1 teaspoon crushed red pepper

2 tablespoons chopped fresh parsley

Plain breadcrumbs, to coat the tops of the fillets (optional)

1. Preheat the oven to 400 degrees.

2. Place the salmon fillets skin side down (if the skin hasn't been removed) in a glass or stainless-steel baking pan large enough to hold them in a single layer. Combine the remaining ingredients except the breadcrumbs. Spoon the mixture over the salmon to coat it evenly, making sure you see the parsley and garlic resting on the salmon. Coat the tops of the fillets with the breadcrumbs. Cover the pan with aluminum foil and cook the salmon in the preheated oven for approximately 15 minutes. Check to see if it's done by inserting a fork into the thickest part of a fillet. Place the tines to your lips for a moment; if it's warm to hot, put the salmon under the broiler for a minute or two to color them lightly. If the fork is cool to cold, return the fish to the oven for another 5 minutes and check again. I love this recipe, and I hope you will, too!

# Sole Oreganata

**I love to make this dish because it's so very simple, tasty, and quick. The broth that's left in the pan after cooking the sole is *deee-licious*. If you're in a rush and you want something really flavorful, give this a try. Jimmy Mulligan, L-156, whose rice pudding recipe is on page 181, kept bothering me to give him this one. That's a real compliment.**

SERVES 4   PREPARATION TIME 15 minutes   COOKING TIME 20 minutes

I cup plain breadcrumbs

½ cup freshly grated Romano cheese

3 cloves garlic, minced

2 tablespoons chopped fresh parsley

2 teaspoons dried oregano

I teaspoon salt

Freshly ground black pepper, to taste

6 tablespoons extra-virgin olive oil

8 (4- to 6-ounce) sole fillets

½ cup dry white wine

½ (8-ounce) bottle clam broth or 8 ounces fresh clam broth

2 lemons sliced into wedges, for garnish

1. Preheat the oven to 400 degrees.

2. In a large mixing bowl, combine the breadcrumbs, cheese, garlic, parsley, oregano, salt, and pepper. Add the olive oil and mix slowly to produce a moist breadcrumb mixture. Place the whiter flesh of the fish face down. If the fillets are very large, slice them in half lengthwise. Spoon the seasoned breadcrumbs over the fillets to coat them evenly, and, starting at the widest part, roll them up with the breadcrumbs on the inside. Arrange the rolled fillets in a baking dish so they are close together but not touching. Add the white wine and the clam broth to the pan, and distribute the remainder of the breadcrumbs on top of the fillets. Bake uncovered in the preheated oven for 20 minutes, until the breadcrumbs turn golden brown and the fillets are cooked through. When they are done, transfer the fillets to individual plates or a serving platter, ladle the broth remaining in the pan over them, and garnish with the lemon wedges. You are going to love this.

# Pan-Seared Tuna

**During the summer months my wife and I eat this dish at least once a week. It's light, easy to make, and one of her favorite dishes.**

SERVES 2   PREPARATION TIME 5 minutes   COOKING TIME 5 minutes

**3 tablespoons sesame oil**

**2 (8-ounce) sushi-quality tuna steaks, sliced about ¾-inch thick with the blood line removed**

**Kosher salt and freshly ground black pepper, to taste**

**2 tablespoons Japanese wasabi powder mixed with 2 tablespoons water**

**2 tablespoons jarred pickled ginger slices, drained**

**Good-quality soy sauce, for dipping**

Place a large skillet, preferably cast iron, over medium-high heat and brush it with 1 tablespoon sesame oil. Brush each tuna steak with about 1 tablespoon sesame oil and season with liberal grindings of black pepper (I coat them almost entirely in pepper) and a bit of kosher salt. Place the steaks in the hot pan, sear them for approximately 2 to 3 minutes on each side, and remove them from the pan. They should be cooked rare to medium. Cut them into ¼-inch-thick slices and serve each one with 1 tablespoon wasabi sauce, 1 tablespoon pickled ginger, and a small bowl of soy sauce for dipping.

# Katsch's Fish and Chips

One winter day at the firehouse, the boys were in the mood for something a little different. Someone suggested fish and chips, and I agreed, but what were we going to use for batter? My friend Bill Katch of L-19 told us what he does when he goes camping with his kids. They use pancake mix, and, guess what, it works! The guys loved it. Actually, Bill has helped me out on more than one occasion—it was he who came with me for the filming of *Cooking Live with Sara Moulton*. He also took the picture of Sara and me.

SERVES 4 to 5  PREPARATION TIME 25 minutes  COOKING TIME 20 minutes

### FOR THE CHIPS

Vegetable oil, for frying

3 pounds russet potatoes, peeled, cut lengthwise into ½-by-½-inch wide strips, and patted dry with paper towels

Salt, to taste

### FOR THE FISH

Prepared pancake mix for 10 to 12 pancakes

Enough dry pancake mix to cover the fish

2 pounds codfish or scrod fillets, cut into 3-inch-by-1-inch pieces

Salt and pepper, to taste

Vegetable oil, for frying (the same oil used to fry the potatoes)

TO MAKE THE CHIPS: Heat the vegetable oil in a pot or a Dutch oven until it reaches 325 degrees. Add the potatoes in small batches to the heated oil. Blanch the potatoes in batches for 4 to 5 minutes until lightly colored, then remove them to a pan lined with paper towels.

1. Reheat the oil to 360 degrees and fry the potatoes in small batches until they are golden brown and crisp. Drain them on fresh paper towels, salt them, and keep them warm, uncovered, in a 250-degree oven until the fish is cooked.

TO COOK THE FISH: Place the prepared pancake mix in one bowl and the dry mix in another. Season the cod with salt and pepper and dip it first in the dry pancake mix to cover the fish completely, and then in the prepared pancake mix. In the same oil you used to fry the chips, cook the fish in small batches at 360 degrees until golden brown. This should take about 3 to 4 minutes. Check one piece of fish to make sure it's cooked all the way through.

2. Serve immediately, with ketchup and/or tartar sauce, or HP Malt Vinegar if you're trying to be very British.

## Safety Tips for Deep or Shallow Pan Frying

WARNING: Cooking oil turns into fuel and could easily burst into flames if overheated or left unattended, causing at worst serious burns or at least damage to your kitchen.

Never leave oil unattended while heating.

Always heat oil carefully, uncovered, on medium heat.

If the oil begins to make smoke, reduce the heat immediately.

Never refill a bottle with hot oil.

IF OIL CATCHES ON FIRE:

Never, ever put water on hot or flaming oil. If you do, you'll create a volcano that spatters oil over everything—possibly including you.

Turn off the heat immediately.

To be sure it doesn't reignite, cover the pot until the oil has cooled to room temperature.

Do not attempt to pick up or carry the pot until the oil has cooled down.

# My Mom's Shrimp Scampi

This way of preparing shrimp scampi is easier than the classic method, requiring less preparation and cooking time, which is why it works so well at the firehouse. I come from a family of five children, so we didn't eat shrimp very often, but when we did, my mom made it like this and we loved it. In fact, it was my sister Laura's favorite dish. My sister Mary had a handwritten copy of the recipe and gave it to me for this book. Thanks, Mom, we miss you!

SERVES **4** PREPARATION TIME **30 minutes** COOKING TIME **10 minutes**

¼ cup extra-virgin olive oil

¼ cup (½ stick) butter

½ teaspoon dried oregano

2 tablespoons dry white wine

2 tablespoons freshly squeezed lemon juice

6 cloves fresh garlic, minced

½ teaspoon salt

Freshly ground black pepper, to taste

2 tablespoons chopped fresh parsley

2 pounds medium shrimp, peeled and deveined

1. Preheat the oven to 350 degrees.

2. Heat the oil and butter in a saucepan over medium heat. Remove the pan from the heat and add the oregano, wine, lemon juice, garlic, salt, pepper, and parsley. Taste the sauce and adjust the seasonings if necessary. Mix the shrimp with the garlic butter, lay them on their sides in a baking dish, and gently pour the leftover scampi butter over them. Cook in the preheated oven for 10 minutes and serve with lots of good Italian bread to sop up the sauce.

The kids and I enjoying a scrumptious meal at the 2001 Ronzoni Marathon Pasta
Party at Tavern on the Green

# Main Course Pastas and Sauces

Italians usually serve a small portion of pasta as a first course, and Americans love pasta as a side dish, but the recipes in this chapter are all hearty enough to be main courses in themselves. A simple salad first, a good crusty bread, a bottle of wine if you like (and if you're not on duty in the firehouse), and you're good to go!

# Fettuccine Alfredo

**Although it certainly isn't fat free, this version is definitely lower in calories and cholesterol than the classic recipe. It's great as an appetizer or as a side dish for parties, and sometimes the guys at the firehouse like to have it as a main course with grilled chicken on top.**

SERVES **4**   PREPARATION TIME **5 minutes**   COOKING TIME **10 minutes**

1½ cups 2% fat milk

1 (8-ounce) package ⅓ reduced-fat cream cheese

1 cup freshly grated Romano cheese, plus additional for sprinkling

Salt and freshly ground black pepper, to taste

1 pound fettuccine noodles or other type of pasta, cooked al dente

1. Combine the milk and cream cheese in a stainless-steel saucepan over a low to medium heat. Stir with a wire whisk for approximately 2 to 3 minutes, until it becomes a smooth sauce. Make sure the sauce doesn't boil, or it will curdle. Whisk in the Romano cheese and season with salt and pepper. Drain the noodles, place them in a large bowl, and mix in the sauce gently but thoroughly. Twirl a portion of noodles onto a large roasting fork and transfer them to a dinner plate. Sprinkle with more Romano and a grinding of pepper, if you wish, and dig in.

2. If you're serving this at a party, place the sauced noodles in a large pasta bowl and sprinkle the Romano and black pepper on top.

# Pasta with Garlic and Oil

This simple sauce can be used with any type of pasta, although it's most commonly served with linguine.

SERVES **3 to 4**    PREPARATION TIME **10 minutes**    COOKING TIME **15 minutes**

I pound linguine, or your favorite pasta

3 cloves garlic, chopped

¾ cup extra-virgin olive oil

¼ teaspoon crushed red pepper

½ teaspoon dried oregano

I teaspoon kosher salt

I tablespoon chopped fresh Italian parsley

½ cup reserved pasta water

Grated zest of I lemon (optional)

1.  Place a large pot of salted water over high heat. When the water comes to a boil, cook linguine until al dente according to package directions.

2.  While the pasta is cooking, set a large sauté pan over medium-high heat and sauté the garlic in the oil for a few minutes, until it just starts to turn golden. Don't burn it or it will become bitter. Remove the pan from the heat and add the crushed red pepper, oregano, and salt. Remove ½ cup pasta water and set it aside. When the pasta is al dente, drain it and return it to the pot along with the hot garlic and oil, the parsley, reserved water, and the lemon zest. Toss it gently and serve immediately.

# Penne Rigati with Summer Vegetables

My sister-in-law Barbara Smith inspired me when she made a version of this dish, and I reworked it for the Ronzoni Firefighters Pasta Cook-Off in 2002. I was lucky enough to be chosen as one of the winners. As a result, it became one of three pasta recipes served to the runners at the Ronzoni Pasta Party held at Tavern on the Green the night before the New York City Marathon. In addition to that honor, Ronzoni donated $10,000 to the Burn Center at Cornell Medical Center and the Uniformed Firefighters Association Widows and Orphans Fund in my name and gave my firehouse a year's supply of pasta.

**SERVES 4**   **PREPARATION TIME** 20 minutes   **COOKING TIME** 20 minutes

I large onion, sliced

1/3 cup extra-virgin olive oil

4 cloves garlic, chopped

3 tablespoons tomato paste

1/3 cup cold water

I pound zucchini, diced into 1/2-inch cubes (about 3 cups)

I pound eggplant, diced into 1/2-inch cubes (about 3 cups)

I pound Ronzoni penne rigati

2 cups cherry tomatoes, halved

I teaspoon kosher salt

I teaspoon crushed red pepper

1/4 cup chopped fresh parsley

1/4 cup chopped fresh basil

1/3 pound ricotta salata or feta cheese, thinly sliced

1. In a large pot, bring 4 quarts cold, salted water to a boil.

2. In a large sauté pan over medium-high heat, sauté the onion in the oil for about 5 minutes, until it is translucent. Add the garlic, sauté for another minute, then cover the onion and garlic with the tomato paste and sauté another 30 seconds. Add the 1/3 cup cold water, turn up the heat, and scrape up any browned bits clinging to the bottom of the pan. Return

the heat to medium-high, add the zucchini and eggplant, cover the pan, and cook for another 10 minutes or so, stirring occasionally. While the zucchini and eggplant are cooking, add the penne to the boiling salted water, and cook it al dente according to package directions. Add the cherry tomatoes, salt, and crushed red pepper to the zucchini and eggplant mixture and cook for another 5 minutes, then remove from the heat. Drain the pasta and quickly run it under cold water to stop the cooking process. Return the pasta to the pot and add the cooked vegetables, the parsley, and the basil. Mix gently to combine the ingredients and serve in large bowls or on individual plates, garnished with the cheese.

# Penne with Chicken and Broccoli

I like to make this dish for lunch at the firehouse, but it works just as well at dinnertime. The chicken broth adds flavor without adding fat. My version is also slightly spicy. The recipe can halved, doubled, tripled, or whatever to serve as many or as few as you wish. Richie Flynn of L-156 says it's his favorite firehouse dish.

SERVES 6 to 8    PREPARATION TIME 20 minutes    COOKING TIME 30 minutes

½ cup extra-virgin olive oil

2 pounds chicken cutlets, trimmed, rinsed, sliced in half lengthwise, and pounded

1 cup flour

6 cloves garlic, minced

1 cup sun-dried tomatoes, sliced (optional)*

1 teaspoon dried oregano

2 (15½-ounce) cans low-sodium chicken broth

½ to 1 teaspoon crushed red pepper (depending how spicy you like it)

8 cups broccoli florets, about 1½-inch square

2 pounds penne (or rigatoni or whatever pasta you prefer)

1 cup reserved pasta water

Salt, to taste

¼ cup chopped fresh parsley

1 cup freshly grated Romano cheese

In a large pot, bring 2 gallons cold, salted water to a boil. Heat the oil in a large sauté pan over medium-high heat. Dredge the chicken cutlets in the flour. When the oil is hot enough so that a pinch of flour sizzles upon contact, add the cutlets and sauté, in batches if necessary, until they are golden brown on both sides, about 2 to 3 minutes per side. Set them aside as they're done, and when all the chicken is browned, add the garlic to the pan. After 1 or 2 minutes, when the garlic starts to turn golden, add the sun-dried tomatoes, oregano, and chicken broth. Set the pan aside over very low heat to barely simmer the broth. Add the broccoli to the pot of boiling water and cook for 2 to 3 minutes, until

*In place of the sun-dried tomatoes, you can also add 1 cup cherry tomatoes, halved, at the end of the cooking time.

it is just al dente and still bright green. Remove it from the pot with a slotted spoon and plunge it immediately into a bowl of ice water to stop the cooking and set the color. *Do not pour the water out of the pot to drain the broccoli.* You will be using it again to cook the pasta. When the water returns to a boil, add the pasta and cook it al dente according to package directions. While the pasta is cooking, slice the chicken into strips, and when the pasta is almost done, turn the heat under the broth to medium high. Once the broth is simmering nicely, add the chicken strips and cook them about 1 minute. Drain the broccoli and add to the broth along with 1 cup pasta water. Add salt to taste and the parsley. Gently combine the broccoli and chicken together and set them aside. Drain the pasta, and run it quickly under cold water to stop the cooking process. Return it to the pot, add the chicken and broccoli mixture, stir gently, and serve immediately with the Romano cheese on the side.

# Penne Alla Vodka

**In the firehouse, it seems that everybody likes a good alla vodka sauce. There are lots of recipes for this, and they are all pretty good. I use bacon in mine, but you could also substitute pancetta or prosciutto, and if you're watching your calories, you can use evaporated skim milk instead of the cream.**

SERVES 6 to 8    PREPARATION TIME 20 minutes    COOKING TIME 45 minutes

¼ pound bacon, diced (You could also use pancetta or prosciutto.)

¼ cup extra-virgin olive oil

6 cloves garlic, peeled and halved

I medium onion, diced

½ cup vodka

2 (28-ounce) cans whole tomatoes, with their juice, puréed in a blender

I teaspoon crushed red pepper

Salt, to taste

I cup heavy cream or 1½ cups evaporated skim milk (for a leaner version)

2 (16-ounce) boxes penne pasta

24 fresh basil leaves, chopped

1½ cups freshly grated Romano cheese

1. Place a large pot of cold, salted water over high heat to come to a boil.

2. In a large sauté pan on medium heat, cook and render fat from the bacon. (If you are using pancetta or prosciutto, skip this step and just sauté it with the garlic.) Once the bacon is almost crisp, remove it from the pan and set it aside. Do not clean the pan. Add the olive oil and, when it is hot, return the bacon to the pan along with the garlic. Sauté until the garlic turns light golden brown, then add the onion and sauté until it becomes translucent, about 5 minutes. Add the vodka and let it reduce by half, then add the tomatoes, red pepper, and salt. Simmer the sauce uncovered for about 30 minutes, stirring occasionally, then add the heavy cream and simmer another 10 minutes. Once you've added the cream, put the pasta in the boiling water and cook until al dente according to package directions. Remove the sauce from the heat, add the basil and the cheese, and stir well. Drain the pasta, shock it with a little cold water, and return it to the pot it was cooked in. Pour the sauce over the pasta and mix gently until the pasta is coated completely. Serve immediately.

# Rigatoni Bolognese

When you're in the mood for something a little different, try this hearty, creamy, meaty sauce with a bit of a bite. I love a good Bolognese sauce over pasta; just give me a pillow to lay my head on when I'm done eating.

SERVES 6    PREPARATION TIME 30 minutes    COOKING TIME 1 hour

4 slices bacon

2 tablespoons butter

2 tablespoons extra-virgin olive oil

6 cloves garlic, minced

I medium onion, minced

I stalk celery, minced

I carrot, minced

I cup minced mushrooms

I pound ground beef

I pound sweet Italian sausage, casing removed

½ cup red wine

I cup heavy cream

I (28-ounce) can whole tomatoes, blended or hand crushed

2 pounds rigatoni, or other pasta of your choice

Salt and crushed red pepper, to taste

¼ cup chopped fresh parsley

2 teaspoons chopped fresh thyme

½ cup freshly grated Pecorino Romano cheese, plus additional for sprinkling

Cook the bacon in a large, shallow sauce pot over medium-high heat. Drain the fat into a safe receptacle, return the pan to the stove, and add the butter and olive oil. When the butter has melted, add the garlic and sauté for about I minute, until the garlic turns golden. Add the onion, celery, carrot, and mushrooms and cook 10 to 15 minutes, until the vegetables soften completely and brown slightly. Add the beef and sausage and cook until the meat is slightly browned, about 10 more minutes. Add the wine and reduce for a few minutes. Add the heavy cream and reduce again for a few minutes. Add the tomatoes and simmer for about 30 minutes. While the sauce is simmering, bring a large pot of cold, salted water to a boil and cook the pasta. Season the sauce with salt and crushed red pepper to taste. When the pasta is almost cooked al dente, add the parsley, thyme, and cheese to the sauce and let it sit for a minute. Drain the pasta and splash some cold water over it to stop the cooking process. Sauce the pasta, sprinkle a little bit of Romano cheese over the top, and serve.

# Rigatoni in a Sauce Alla Fresca

This is the first pasta dish I created for the Ronzoni Firefighters Pasta Cook-Off. I was chosen as one of the three finalists, and Ronzoni donated $10,000 in each of our names to the Uniformed Firefighters Widows and Orphans Fund and the Burn Center at Cornell Medical Center.

SERVES 4 to 5    PREPARATION TIME 30 minutes    COOKING TIME 15 minutes

½ cup extra-virgin olive oil

9 cloves garlic, peeled and halved

2 fresh cayenne peppers, chopped, or 3 teaspoons crushed red pepper

1 pound lean bacon

1 medium Bermuda onion, diced

4 medium plum tomatoes, diced, or 2 (28-ounce) cans crushed tomatoes

1 (1-pound) box rigatoni

1 (15-ounce) jar artichoke hearts, packed in water, drained, and cut in quarters

⅓ cup roughly chopped basil

Salt and pepper, to taste

1 cup grated Locatelli Romano cheese

Place olive oil, garlic, and cayenne peppers in a small saucepan and sauté over medium heat until the garlic starts to brown. Remove the pan from the heat and set it aside. In a large saucepot, bring 5 quarts cold water and 2 teaspoons salt to a boil. While the water is coming to a boil, cook the bacon in a large skillet and set it aside to drain on paper towels. Drain all the grease from the skillet into a safe receptacle but *do not wash the pan*. The pan will retain the flavor of the bacon without all the fat. Drain the garlic and peppers from the oil and discard them. Add the oil to the pan in which you cooked the bacon. When the oil is hot, add the onion and sauté over medium heat until it is translucent. Then add the chopped bacon, the tomatoes, and the artichoke hearts and bring the mixture to a simmer.

Whenever you're cooking, even if you're just boiling water, always begin with cold water. You'll be less likely to transfer the lead solder that's inside your pipes to your food.

While the sauce is simmering, add the rigatoni to the pot of boiling water and cook uncovered, stirring occasionally to prevent it from sticking, until it is just al dente, approximately 14 minutes. Drain the pasta and shock it with cold water to stop the cooking process. Add the chopped basil and salt and pepper to taste to the tomato sauce and remove it from the heat. Ladle this fresh and delicious sauce over the rigatoni, serve the cheese on the side, and enjoy.

# My Marinara Sauce

To make a good marinara sauce you have to start with good tomatoes. Finding a good tomato product can involve a bit of trial and error. Look for canned tomatoes with no citric acid or calcium chloride added. When I make a sauce at home, I usually use whole plum tomatoes and crush them by hand. If you like the tomatoes more finely chopped, you can pulse them in a blender for a few seconds.

SERVES 5 to 6    PREPARATION TIME 10 minutes    COOKING TIME 45 minutes

6 large cloves garlic, peeled and minced

½ cup extra-virgin olive oil

1 medium onion, diced

3 (28-ounce) cans whole plum tomatoes, hand crushed or blended

6 leaves fresh basil, chopped

Salt, to taste

½ teaspoon crushed red pepper, or to taste

In a large saucepan over medium-high heat, sauté the garlic in the oil for 2 to 3 minutes, until it starts to turn golden. Add the onion and sauté until it becomes translucent, about 5 minutes. Add the tomatoes, bring the sauce to a simmer, and continue to simmer for about 30 minutes. Add the basil, salt, and crushed red pepper, and simmer another 5 minutes. Taste the sauce and adjust the seasonings. Now it's ready to serve over your favorite pasta or to use as the base for another delicious sauce such as puttanesca or Alla Vodka (page 128).

When cooking any tomato products, try not to use aluminum pots or pans. The acid in the tomato product reacts with the aluminum in the pan. If that's all that you have to cook in, use wooden spoons, not metal, for stirring. The stainless steel of the metal utensil is harder than the aluminum of the pan and will scrape up the aluminum, which will wind up in your food.

# Pesto

Making pesto is a great and delicious way to make use of the overabundant basil in your garden. But if you don't have a garden, you can still enjoy pesto. Fresh basil is readily available in most supermarkets and produce stands. Some of the guys at the firehouse love this and some, like Lieutenant Kevin Kennedy, don't want to touch it because they hate anything that's green.

MAKES approximately 4½ cups    PREPARATION TIME 15 minutes

2 cups fresh basil leaves

1¼ cups extra-virgin olive oil

⅓ cup lightly toasted pignoli nuts

1 cup freshly grated Romano cheese

1 clove garlic, roughly chopped

½ teaspoon salt

¼ teaspoon crushed red pepper

Combine all the ingredients in a blender and pulse until the mixture becomes a fine paste. Toss it with a pound of your favorite pasta, or freeze it in small batches to use when you need a touch of summer freshness in the dead of winter.

# Sun-Dried Tomato Pesto with Fresh Rosemary

This simple recipe can be made ahead of time and stored for up to one month in the refrigerator in a sealed container. The pesto can be tossed with a pound of freshly cooked pasta; it can be added to any tomato-based sauce for an extra boost of flavor; or it can be used as a spread for a variety of sandwiches. Try it and find your own use for it.

MAKES 4½ cups   PREPARATION TIME 15 minutes

2 cups sun-dried tomatoes packed in oil

1 clove garlic, roughly chopped

1½ cups extra-virgin olive oil

2 tablespoons finely chopped fresh rosemary

1 cup freshly grated Romano cheese

2 tablespoons salt

¼ teaspoon crushed red pepper

Combine the sun-dried tomatoes, garlic, olive oil, and rosemary in a blender and pulse until the tomatoes become a fine paste. Transfer the mixture to a bowl and add the Romano cheese, salt, and crushed red pepper. Stir to combine, and the pesto is ready to use.

It's 5 P.M. and the guys are exhausted after finally finishing building inspections with (left to right) John Sullivan, Lieutenant Smith, George Storz, Jimmy Mulligan, Richie "the Neckcracker" Flynn, and Arsen Kasparian, L-156

# Vegetables and Other Side Dishes

If the main dish itself has complex flavors and components, the only accompaniment it might need is a simply steamed green vegetable or a baked potato. Many of my firefighting brothers probably wouldn't care if I never served them a vegetable at all, but they certainly love their starches, and a simple rice or noodle dish can serve not only to "stretch" the meal but also to sop up all the delicious sauce from a brisket or a chicken cacciatore.

These are a few of my own favorite "sides" and the ones that have won the approval of my fussy brothers at the station.

# Broccoli and Corn Succotash

Succotash is usually made with lima or cranberry beans and corn, but I like this variation. It's a light and bright vegetable dish with an array of different colors that goes well with almost any meal.

SERVES 5 to 6    PREPARATION TIME 15 minutes    COOKING TIME 12 to 15 minutes

I (1½-pound) head of broccoli, washed and cut into 1-inch florets (about 5 or 6 cups)

3 tablespoons olive oil

I red bell pepper, seeded and diced

I medium onion, diced

3 cloves garlic, minced

2 cups frozen corn

I teaspoon freshly grated lemon zest

Salt and freshly ground black pepper, to taste

Juice of ¼ lemon (optional)

Blanch the broccoli in a large pot of boiling water for approximately 3 minutes. Drain and immediately plunge into ice water to stop the cooking process. Set the broccoli aside. Heat the olive oil in a large skillet over medium-high heat. Add the red bell pepper, onion, and garlic and sauté approximately 6 minutes, stirring constantly, until the vegetables are soft. Add the corn and cook for another 3 minutes, until hot. Add the lemon zest and broccoli and cook until the broccoli is warmed through, approximately 2 to 3 minutes. Season with salt and pepper and, if you like, drizzle with lemon juice just before serving.

# Rob "Angel One" Angelone

Don't be fooled by the nickname—Rob's no angel. He's a good friend and a hardworking guy but when it comes to food, Rob can be a little peculiar. It always makes me laugh to hear him insist that bacon is his favorite vegetable. Rob and vegetables just don't mix. The closest I've ever seen him come to eating one is when he devours a bag of corn chips. He doesn't look out of shape to me, but lately he's been complaining that his head looks too large in photographs and he's going to have to go on a diet. At least he can laugh at himself!

He's also a guy with a great imagination, which might be the reason he's the only one in the firehouse to have seen a ghost. One night in the bunkroom, he told me, he saw an old fireman dressed in an ancient turnout coat, helmet, and boots. He just chalked it up to having eaten too much junk food—but then it happened again. This time, seeing the "ghost" standing at the foot of his bed scared him so much that he pulled the covers over his head and waited until he thought the ghost had gone. But when he finally poked his head out, it was still there. He ducked under the covers again and waited until he heard the bunkroom door open and close. This time, when he looked, the ghost was gone—and so was Rob. He refused to sleep in the bunkroom again for about a year.

The third time he saw the ghost, I was on duty, too. Rob was sleeping diagonally across from me when I heard him get out of bed and shout, "What's up?" in a voice loud enough to raise the dead. Then he just walked out of the bunkroom. He told me later that he'd tried to tackle the ghost but had just run right through him.

I told him the ghost was probably trying to send him a message: "Eat your broccoli!"

JERRY RUOTOLO

Rob Angelone, E-276, describing to firehouse guest Sarah Chumsky what broccoli tastes like to him

# Chick Peas with Chorizo Sausage

**This quick and delicious recipe is low in fat and high in protein.**

⅓ cup olive oil

1 medium onion, diced

½ green bell pepper, seeded and diced

3 cloves garlic, minced

3 chorizo sausages, thinly sliced (I like Goya.)

½ cup tomato sauce or stewed tomatoes

2 (15-ounce) cans chick peas with their liquid

2 tablespoons chopped fresh cilantro

Heat the oil in a large saucepan over medium-high heat. Add the onion and green bell pepper and sauté until the onion is translucent and the pepper softens, about 5 minutes. Add the garlic and sausage and sauté 1 more minute. Add the tomato sauce and chick peas and bring to a slow boil. Lower the heat and simmer for 20 to 25 minutes. Add the cilantro, give the contents of the pan a good stir, and serve it as a side dish with Pernil (page 96). You can also serve this over rice and make a meal of it. You decide.

Vegetables and Other Side Dishes

# Gandules and Rice

The first time I ever tasted this delicious rice dish was at my friend Kris Andreassen's house when he was giving yet another one of his endless parties. You can reheat this in the microwave a day or two after it's cooked and it will still be just as good as when you first made it. I love to serve it with Pernil (page 96).

SERVES 8 to 10   PREPARATION TIME 15 minutes   COOKING TIME 40 minutes

3 tablespoons extra-virgin olive oil

1 packet Goya Sazon with cilantro and achiote

2 teaspoons distilled white vinegar

2 tablespoons Goya Adobo seasoning

1 teaspoon dried oregano

6 cloves garlic, finely chopped

2 tablespoons chopped fresh cilantro

1 (16-ounce) can gandules (pigeon peas), drained, liquid reserved

3½ cups long-grain white rice

Combine the olive oil, Goya Sazon, vinegar, Goya Adobo seasoning, oregano, garlic, and cilantro in a food processor and process to the consistency of a thick salad dressing. Transfer the mixture to a large pot, set it over medium-high heat, and simmer for approximately 1 minute. Measure the liquid from the gandules and add enough cold water to make 5½ cups liquid. Add this to the pot along with the gandules and bring to a boil. Add the rice, return to a boil, then lower the heat and simmer for 10 minutes, stirring the rice occasionally. After 10 minutes, stir the rice one last time, lower the heat so the rice doesn't burn, cover, and cook for 20 to 25 minutes. When the rice has finished cooking, stir it once more to break the steam seal so the rice won't overcook and get sticky. When you taste this rice I assure you, there will be no disappointment. Try not eating it all in one sitting.

VARIATION: **Brown rice also works well in this dish, and in fact I prefer it. Just substitute 3½ cups brown rice for the white rice, and use 7 cups liquid, including the liquid reserved from the gandules. Cook the rice for 40 to 45 minutes.**

# Orzo with Onions and Teriyaki

This is another of my mother-in-law's famous recipes that's gotten the seal of approval from the guys at the firehouse. She used to serve it on Sunday afternoons with G'ma's Zucchini Pie (page 150), marinated London broil, and a salad.

**SERVES 4 to 6    PREPARATION TIME 10 minutes    COOKING TIME 20 minutes**

1 (1-pound) box orzo

¼ cup extra-virgin olive oil

1 medium yellow onion, diced

3 cloves garlic, minced

10 ounces white mushrooms, sliced

¼ cup teriyaki sauce

⅛ cup soy sauce

¼ teaspoon crushed red pepper

Set a pot of cold, salted water over high heat and, when it comes to a boil, cook the orzo until al dente according to package directions. Meanwhile, heat the oil in a large sauté pan over medium-high heat. Sauté the onion in the hot oil until translucent, about 5 minutes. Add the garlic and mushrooms to the pan and sauté until the mushrooms start to lose their moisture and reduce in size, about 5 more minutes. Remove the pan from the heat, and add the teriyaki sauce, soy sauce, and crushed red pepper. When the orzo is cooked al dente, drain, add it to the sauté pan, and stir gently to combine the ingredients. This can be served immediately or held for up to 30 minutes—it tastes good either way.

Vegetables and Other Side Dishes

# Pa's Fried Plantains

**My brothers Jeffrey and Duane told me I absolutely had to put my grandfather's plantain recipe in my cookbook. My grandfather used to visit us a couple times a year, and we loved those visits because he always cooked and we loved the food that he made. These go well with Pernil (page 96) and Gandules and Rice (page 141).**

SERVES **4**   PREPARATION TIME **5 minutes**   COOKING TIME **20 to 25 minutes**

**1½ cups vegetable oil (My grandfather used lard.)**

**2 green or yellow plantains, peeled and cut into 1-inch pieces (The green ones are not sweet; the yellow ones are.)**

**Kosher salt, to taste**

Heat the oil in a large heavy skillet over medium-high heat. When the oil is hot enough that a small piece of bread sizzles when it's dropped in, fry the plantains in batches for about 3 or 4 minutes on each side. When they're all done, place them on a cutting board and squash them with a plate or a spatula. Return the squashed plantains to the oil and fry them another 2 to 3 minutes on each side. Drain them on paper towels, season with kosher salt, and serve immediately.

# Food Fight with the Cops

The Food Network debuted a new program in 2003 called *Food Fight*.

I was chosen, along with my best friend, Dave McAndrews of E-289, to face off against a couple of New York city police.

For days—and nights—before the cookoff I dreamed about food and cooking. I had a lot at stake—not money but my reputation. If I lost, I'd be razzed by the guys at the firehouse for the rest of my life. Did I really want to be known as the guy who lost to the cops on *Food Fight*?

The filming was scheduled for January 12. I didn't sleep well the night before, and I had to be up at 5 A.M. to get to Tavern on the Green, where the show was being filmed, by 7 A.M. On these kinds of shows you never know what the main ingredient will be. As it turned out, it was bone-in NY cut shell steak, which relieved a lot of my anxiety. This was something I knew how to work with. Dave and I made Steak au Poivre with a Mushroom, Green Peppercorn, Dijon Sauce (page 91), Pommes Frites with Aioli Dipping Sauce (page 145), and a Raw Vegetable Relish Timbale (page 163). I can't say that the shopping and cooking weren't stressful, but I was happy with the way our dish turned out, and luckily the judges agreed.

Dave and I won! The guys would have to wait for me to screw up another time.

JERRY RUOTOLO

"Getting a bite" before filming the "Food Fight" segment for The Food Network

# Pommes Frites with Aioli Dipping Sauce

*Pommes frites* is the French way to say French fries—French fries the way I make them, anyway. These are easy to make as long as you're careful when you're frying. When we made these for *Food Fight,* the kitchen we were working in was very tight for space. My buddy Dave accidentally left a kitchen towel too close to the flame, and, when it caught on fire, everyone watching the show got to see a couple very embarrassed firefighters trying to blow it out. Cameras were rolling; they caught it all on tape. Please learn from our mistakes.

The aioli dipping sauce is delicious and made a nice contrast on the plate. We garnished the sauce with some chopped chives for a little extra color.

MAKES **2 large servings**    PREPARATION TIME **10 minutes**    COOKING TIME **20 minutes**

### FOR THE POTATOES

**6 cups vegetable oil**

**3 large russet or Yukon gold potatoes, peeled and sliced into ½-by-½-inch sticks**

### FOR THE DIPPING SAUCE

**4 fresh egg yolks**

**I clove garlic**

**I tablespoon freshly squeezed lemon juice**

**¾ cup olive oil**

**Kosher salt and freshly ground black pepper, to taste**

TO MAKE THE POMMES FRITES: Heat the vegetable oil in a large pot over medium-high heat. When the oil is hot enough (test it by dropping in a potato slice and seeing if it sizzles; if it doesn't, wait a minute or two and try again; don't let the oil get any hotter than 360 degrees), add half the potatoes and fry them 4 to 5 minutes, just until they start to brown around the edges. Remove them with a slotted spoon and drain on paper towels. Repeat with the rest of the potatoes. Turn off the heat under the oil.

TO MAKE THE SAUCE: Combine the egg yolks, garlic, and lemon juice in a blender and process until the mixture is frothy and the garlic is completely liquefied, about I minute. With the blender running, add the olive oil slowly in a steady stream for about 2 more minutes. Season with salt and pepper and set aside.

TO FINISH THE POTATOES: Reheat the oil and refry the potatoes for approximately 2 minutes, until they are golden brown. Drain again on paper towels, season with salt and pepper, and serve immediately with the aioli dipping sauce on the side.

NOTE **The aioli is made with raw egg so if you are concerned then you'll have to forgo this dipping sauce.**

# Baked and Buttered Spaghetti Squash

**Spaghetti squash is a versatile and colorful vegetable. I like to use it as a bed for a variety of entrées, such as Short Ribs of Beef with Pepperoncini (page 86). When it's cooked, the flesh can be spooned out of the skin in strands that look very much like spaghetti. This dish reheats well, and its flavor can be changed by adding various ingredients such as diced tomato, chopped basil, and minced garlic to the mixture.**

SERVES 6 to 7    PREPARATION TIME 5 minutes    COOKING TIME 1 hour

**1 (4- to 5-pound) spaghetti squash, rinsed and cut in half (Cutting it in half evenly is the hardest part of making this dish.)**

**1½ cups cold water**

**6 tablespoons butter**

**Kosher salt and freshly ground black pepper, to taste**

1.  Preheat the oven to 350 degrees.

2.  Place the squash flesh side down in an ovenproof baking pan. Add the cold water to the pan and bake the squash in the preheated oven for approximately 1 hour or until the skin pulls easily away from the flesh. Remove the squash from the oven and, after about 5 minutes when it's cool enough to handle, spoon all the flesh into a large mixing bowl. Add the butter and mix gently until all the butter has melted. Salt and pepper the squash to your taste and serve it as a side dish or use it as a bed for fish or beef stew.

# Firehouse Guests

Sometimes a firefighter or officer invites a guest or guests to share our meal. We never have a problem with that. We just buy more food, and usually we pay for the guest's meal.

If it's a male guest over the age of 10, he's treated like one of the men. He picks up his meal with the guys and sits down with the guys. Women and children are treated a bit differently. We usually seat them and bring them their silverware and plated food.

We try to keep our guests entertained, and hopefully it's an enjoyable experience for everyone involved.

JERRY RUOTOLO

Every woman's fantasy, a man who will cook, serve, and clean up. The lucky women are (left to right) Sarah Chumsky, Susan Chumsky, and Meg Bowles. Susan was at the firehouse to interview me for *O: The Oprah Magazine*

# Teriyaki String Beans with Onions and Mushrooms

**These beans are easy, and great to serve with almost any meat, poultry, or fish dish, either in the firehouse or at home.**

SERVES 6   PREPARATION TIME **15 minutes**   COOKING TIME **20 minutes**

**2 tablespoons butter**

**2 tablespoons olive oil**

**I large onion, sliced**

**3 cloves garlic, peeled and minced**

**10 ounces white mushrooms, sliced**

**2 pounds fresh string beans, rinsed, topped, and tailed**

**Approximately ½ cup teriyaki sauce (You can use a bit more or less to suit your taste.)**

**Salt and freshly ground black pepper, to taste**

1. Bring 4 quarts water and 1 tablespoon salt to a boil in a large pot. While the water is coming to the boil, heat the butter and olive oil in a large sauté pan over medium-high heat and, when the butter has melted, add the onion and sauté until it is translucent, about 5 minutes. Add the garlic and sauté another 2 minutes, then add the mushrooms and continue to sauté for another 10 minutes, stirring frequently.

2. While the mushrooms and onions are cooking, the water should have come to a boil. Add the string beans and cook for 3 to 4 minutes. The string beans should be bright green and still slightly crisp; they should not be limp and mushy. Drain the string beans through a colander and add them directly to the pan with the other ingredients along with the teriyaki sauce, salt, and pepper. Cook for 3 minutes on low heat and serve immediately.

# G'ma's Zucchini Pie

My mother-in-law used to make this dish very often for Sunday dinner in the summer, and now John "Freddy" Horan of E-319 makes it all the time, too. I've always loved it. It can be served either as an appetizer or as a side dish.

SERVES 8    PREPARATION TIME 10 minutes    COOKING TIME 45 minutes

3 cups quartered and sliced zucchini

1 medium onion, diced

1 cup Bisquick

4 eggs

½ cup olive oil

½ cup freshly grated Romano cheese

2 cloves garlic, minced

1 tablespoon chopped fresh parsley

1 tablespoon chopped fresh basil

1 teaspoon crushed red pepper (optional)

1. Preheat the oven to 375 degrees.

2. Combine all the ingredients in a large mixing bowl and mix thoroughly but gently. Place the mixture in a 9-inch round baking dish and bake in the preheated oven until golden brown on top and cooked through, approximately 45 minutes. Cool for about 10 minutes before serving.

# Sautéed Zucchini with Onions and Peppers

This is a fast, colorful, and tasty vegetable dish—and a good way to use up a harvest of zucchini!

SERVES 8   PREPARATION TIME 10 minutes   COOKING TIME 10 minutes

¼ cup olive oil

I large onion, peeled and sliced

3 red bell peppers, cored, sliced lengthwise, and cut in half crosswise

3 cloves garlic, minced

4 medium zucchini, halved lengthwise and sliced crosswise

½ stick (¼ cup) butter, cut up

Salt and freshly ground black pepper, to taste

2 tablespoons chopped fresh parsley

Heat the oil in a large skillet over medium-high heat. Add the onion and red bell peppers and sauté until the onion is translucent, about 6 minutes. Add the garlic and sauté I more minute. Add the zucchini and sauté for 2 to 3 minutes, then add the butter, stirring constantly for another I or 2 minutes. Season with salt and pepper, stir in the parsley, and serve immediately.

# Yummy Grilled Vegetables

This dish is great for summer outdoor grilling, but if you have a craving for yummy vegetables in the dead of winter, you can roast them in the oven.

SERVES 12    PREPARATION TIME 15 minutes    COOKING TIME 20 minutes

1 cup olive oil

1 teaspoon dried oregano

1 tablespoon **Goya Adobo seasoning**, or salt and freshly ground black pepper, to taste

1 eggplant, sliced crosswise into ½-inch-thick rounds

6 zucchini, sliced on the bias into ¾-inch-thick ovals

3 onions, preferably Vidalia, cut into 6 pieces, leaving the root bottom attached to hold the onion together

3 whole red peppers

1.  Preheat the grill to high.

2.  In a mixing bowl, combine the olive oil, oregano, and Goya Adobo seasoning. Lay the eggplant on a sheet pan and brush both sides with the olive oil mixture. Eggplant is like a sponge, so be careful not to use too much oil, because that would be like putting fuel on the grill. Grill until they are golden brown on both sides and set them aside. Next, do the same with the zucchini and then the onions. Grill the peppers whole, turning to char the skin on all sides. When they're done and cool enough to handle, strip off the skin (it will peel away easily), halve and seed the peppers, and cut them into strips. Arrange all the grilled veggies neatly on a large platter and serve. (I try to get the guys at the firehouse to do this, but have you ever tried to get a fireman to arrange cooked vegetables neatly? They taste just as good, though, however you arrange them.)

To roast the vegetables, preheat the oven to 500 degrees. Core the peppers and cut them into wide strips. Baste both sides of the vegetables with the oil mixture, lay them close together in a single layer in a large roasting pan, and roast for 15 minutes.

# Fool-Proof White Rice

**I find that these proportions work better than the ones you usually get on the box. The rice is fluffier, and the grains are nice and separated.**

SERVES 5 generously   PREPARATION TIME 3 minutes   COOKING TIME 30 minutes

   3½ cups cold water

   2 tablespoons olive oil or butter

   2 teaspoons salt

   2 cups long-grain white rice

Bring the water, oil, and salt to a boil, then add the rice. When the water returns to the boil, reduce the heat and simmer uncovered for 10 minutes, stirring occasionally. Cover and reduce heat slightly, but make sure the rice is still simmering. Cook the rice for another 20 minutes, and give it a stir before serving. Nice and simple.

VARIATIONS  **Stir in these ingredients 5 minutes before rice finishes cooking:**

1. **2 cups raw broccoli florets or asparagus tips and 1 cup grated Romano cheese**

2. **2 cups frozen peas, 3 slices prosciutto, diced, and 1 cup grated Romano or mozzarella cheese**

3. **1 cup frozen peas, 1 small red bell pepper, finely diced, and 1 yellow bell pepper, finely diced**

# Always Perfect Brown Rice

**What makes brown rice brown is the fact that its hull hasn't been removed as it has in white rice. The hull is full of vitamins, minerals, and fiber, which means that brown rice is healthier than white rice. It also takes about twice as long to cook, but for me the result is worth the wait. The directions on the back of the package usually tell you to use 2½ cups water to 1 cup rice, but I find that tends to make the rice a little mushy. Try this recipe; the grains will be separated and the rice will be fluffier. Serve it as a side dish instead of white rice, pasta, or potatoes.**

SERVES 5 generously　PREPARATION TIME 3 minutes　COOKING TIME 50 minutes

4 cups cold water

2 tablespoons olive oil or butter

2 teaspoons salt

2 cups brown rice

Bring the water, oil, and salt to a boil, then add the rice. Return to the boil and simmer uncovered for 10 minutes, stirring to be sure the rice isn't sticking to the bottom of the pan. After 10 minutes, cover the pot and reduce the heat slightly, but make sure the rice is still simmering. Cook 40 minutes without stirring. When the rice is done, stir it to release the steam and serve it.

# Classic Mashed Potatoes

**I learned from Tom Lynch, a senior man at L-19 in the Bronx, that you don't mess with mashed potatoes; they are a perfect food.**

SERVES 5 to 6    PREPARATION TIME 10 minutes    COOKING TIME 20 minutes

**5 pounds russet or Yukon gold potatoes, peeled and cut in 1-inch cubes**

**1 stick (½ cup) butter**

**1 cup sour cream**

**Salt and pepper, to taste**

Place the peeled and cubed potatoes in a large pot with cold water and bring to a boil over high heat, then reduce the heat and simmer for approximately 10 to 15 minutes, until the potatoes are soft but not falling apart. Drain the potatoes and return them to the pot, or transfer them to a stainless-steel mixing bowl if using an aluminum pot. Add the butter and sour cream to the pot and mash until the potatoes are smooth and the ingredients are thoroughly combined. Add the salt and pepper to taste and serve with your favorite roast, stew, or turkey.

# Smashing Sweet Potatoes

**These sweet potatoes make a great holiday side dish to serve with ham or turkey.**

SERVES 8    PREPARATION TIME **15 minutes**    COOKING TIME **15 minutes**

**5 pounds sweet potatoes, peeled and cubed to 1 inch**

**⅓ cup butter**

**⅓ cup brown sugar**

**⅓ cup honey**

**½ teaspoon ground cinnamon**

**½ teaspoon ground allspice**

**Salt and freshly ground black pepper, to taste**

Place the peeled and cubed sweet potatoes in a large pot with cold water and bring a large pot of water to a boil over high heat. Then reduce the heat and simmer for 10 to 15 minutes, until they can be easily pierced with a fork. While the sweet potatoes are simmering, combine the butter and brown sugar in a saucepan over medium heat and cook until the butter melts and the sugar caramelizes. Remove the pan from the heat. When the sweet potatoes are done, drain and mash them, then add the caramelized sugar, honey, cinnamon, allspice, and salt and pepper to taste. The potatoes can be served at once, kept warm in a covered baking dish for about half an hour, or reheated in a microwave, if necessary.

# Creamy Coleslaw

Homemade coleslaw is about 110 percent better than any premade stuff that is mass-produced at a factory somewhere. I love fresh coleslaw with burgers, sandwiches, or at barbecues. This recipe is basic and simple enough to make any time.

SERVES 6 to 8     PREPARATION TIME 20 minutes     MARINATING TIME 30 minutes

1 large (3½-pound) head white cabbage, cored and thinly sliced

½ Vidalia onion, thinly sliced

2 carrots, peeled and shredded

1½ cups mayonnaise

2 tablespoons cider vinegar

2 tablespoons sugar

2 teaspoons kosher salt

2 teaspoons freshly ground black pepper

Combine all the ingredients in a large bowl and mix gently until all the cabbage is covered with a thin coating of dressing. Allow the slaw to marinate in the refrigerator for half an hour before serving.

VARIATIONS

1. Add 1 chopped fresh jalapeño pepper to make it a spicy slaw.
2. Add 1 cup red cabbage to give it a little more color.
3. Add 2 to 3 teaspoons freshly grated ginger to give it a little bite.

# Fresh Slaw

I used to eat this salad when I worked the pantry at a restaurant in my hometown of Freeport, New York. The Latin American cooks and dishwashers made it to serve as a side dish for our employee meals. It was quick and always very refreshing on those hot summer days in the kitchen. It also makes an excellent base for Ceviche (page 11).

SERVES 8 to 10    PREPARATION TIME 10 minutes    MARINATING TIME 10 minutes

I large (3½-pound) head white cabbage, cored and thinly sliced

2 ripe tomatoes, diced

½ Bermuda onion, thinly sliced

¼ cup chopped fresh cilantro

½ cup extra-virgin olive oil

Juice of 1½ to 2 limes (depending upon how tangy you like things)

Salt and freshly ground black pepper, to taste

Gently but thoroughly combine all the ingredients in a large bowl, and let the salad marinate for about 10 minutes before serving.

# Fresh Tomato and Cucumber Salad

Philly Scafuri, Chauffeur E-276, told me that you never put vinegar in a tomato salad. He says that none of the best restaurants in Manhattan ever add vinegar to their tomato salads. Philly also told me that you never ever put any kind of cheese on seafood; he says it's unnatural. He says cows don't swim in the ocean, so why would you put cheese on seafood? He also wants me to tell everyone who's reading this book that he's about 6' 2" even though he's 5' 6" with shoes on.

The best way to make this salad is with tomatoes and cucumbers fresh from your own garden. If you don't have a garden, make sure you buy nothing but vine-ripened tomatoes and nice firm cucumbers.

SERVES 8 to 10    PREPARATION TIME 15 minutes

18 plum tomatoes, diced (about 4 cups)

1 large cucumber, peeled, seeded, quartered, and chopped

½ red onion, diced

3 cloves garlic, peeled and halved (not to be eaten, just used for flavor then discarded)

¼ cup extra-virgin olive oil

2 tablespoons balsamic or red wine vinegar (optional)—sorry, Philly

2 tablespoons chopped fresh basil

Salt and pepper, to taste

Gently mix all the ingredients together in a bowl and serve as a side dish with any meal.

VARIATIONS

1. Add ½ cup feta cheese and some black olives.

2. Add 1 cup diced fresh mozzarella.

3. Top with grilled chicken breast or sautéed shrimp for a light meal.

MICHAEL SALICA E-276

**Phil Scafuri, E-276, getting ready to give me some good advice**

# Homemade Red Potato Salad

This is the perfect salad to serve with hamburgers and hot dogs, with fried chicken, or with any kind of sandwich.

SERVES 12 to 14    PREPARATION TIME 10 minutes    COOKING TIME 20 minutes

5 pounds red potatoes, with their skins on, cut into 1-inch cubes

4 eggs, hard-boiled and diced

1 bunch scallions, white and green parts, chopped

3 carrots, shredded

2 stalks celery, chopped

1 cup mayonnaise

2 tablespoons Dijon mustard

2 tablespoons chopped fresh dill (optional)

2 teaspoons salt

1 teaspoon freshly ground black pepper

Bring the potatoes to a boil in a large pot of cold, salted water. When the water starts to boil, lower the heat and simmer the potatoes for 10 to 12 minutes until they are easily pierced with a fork but not falling apart. When they are done, drain and return them to the pot with cold water and ice to stop the cooking process and hasten cooling. When the potatoes are cold, transfer them to a large mixing bowl and add the rest of the ingredients. Mix gently but thoroughly with a spoon. Cover and refrigerate the salad until you are ready to serve.

# Tabbouleh Salad

The first time I had this delightful salad was in a Mediterranean restaurant. It was tangy and light and reminded me of summer. I went home that night and wrote down the ingredients so I could make it myself. George Storz, L-156, is a tabbouleh connoisseur and always lets me know when I've got mine just right.

SERVES 15    PREPARATION TIME 30 minutes

3 bunches Italian parsley, washed, dried, and finely chopped

1 bunch scallions, green and white parts, washed and chopped

1 Vidalia onion, diced

6 large ripe tomatoes, or 12 ripe plum tomatoes, diced

2 cucumbers, peeled, seeded, and diced

1 (10-ounce) box couscous

¼ cup chopped fresh mint leaves (optional)

Juice of 2 medium lemons

⅓ cup extra-virgin olive oil

Salt and freshly ground black pepper, to taste

Combine the parsley, scallions, onion, tomatoes, and cucumbers in a large pot of cold, salted water and set them aside to soak. While the vegetables are soaking, prepare the couscous according to package directions and, as soon as you've fluffed it, spread it in a sheet pan and put it in the freezer for 10 to 15 minutes. When the couscous is cool, drain the vegetables. Combine all the ingredients in a large bowl and mix gently. The tabbouleh is now ready to serve.

# Timmy Boy's Chopped Salad

The first time I tried this salad, it was at the restaurant where my friend Timmy Branni-gan was working as a chef. I decided to make it at the firehouse one day, and when the guys saw the ingredients, they all started claiming to be out on the meal—meaning they didn't want to help prepare it, pay for it, or eat it—until they tried it, that is. This salad is a delicious and healthy addition to practically any meal.

SERVES 4 to 5    PREPARATION TIME 20 minutes

1 (15½-ounce) can chick peas, drained

3 carrots, peeled and finely diced

2 stalks celery, finely diced

½ Bermuda onion, diced

½ cucumber, peeled, seeded, and diced

2 tablespoons chopped fresh dill

2 tablespoons red wine vinegar or freshly squeezed lemon juice

2 tablespoons extra-virgin olive oil

2 medium ripe tomatoes, diced, or 1 cup cherry tomatoes

½ cup crumbled feta cheese

Salt and freshly ground black pepper, to taste

Pinch of sugar (optional)

In a large mixing bowl, combine all the ingredients except the tomatoes, feta cheese, and black pepper. Just before serving, gently mix in the tomatoes, feta, salt, pepper, and sugar if you like your dressing a bit sweet. (The reason I add these ingredients at the last minute is so the tomatoes don't break down and the feta doesn't turn your salad a milky white.)

VARIATIONS

1. Serve it over a bed of radicchio with grilled chicken on top.

2. To give it a little kick, add 1 chopped fresh jalapeño pepper.

3. Instead of the dill, use 2 tablespoons of your favorite fresh herb, such as parsley, chives, basil, or cilantro. Each one of these herbs will give the salad a different flavor.

4. To make Raw Vegetable Relish Timbale, halve this recipe and omit the chick peas. Press the salad into a small teacup to compress it and drain off the liquid, then turn the cup over onto a plate to unmold the timbale.

The boys, with guest John Sineno, seated second from right, taking a breather and getting a bite

# Desserts

I confess that I don't always make dessert in the firehouse. It's just that much more work. But firefighters seem to have an insatiable sweet tooth, and sometimes you've got to break down and feed the craving. These dessert recipes are great for the firehouse, at home, or for special occasions.

# Grandma's Irish Soda Bread

My kids called her Grandma and I called her Mrs. King. She was my mother-in-law, but she always made me feel like I was part of her family. This is my mother-in-law's quintessential recipe. This is the kind of bread you have with coffee or tea in the morning, or as a snack during the day. Everybody knew and loved Grandma's Irish Soda Bread. She would make it around the holidays, for St. Patrick's Day, or for birthdays. Now you're lucky enough to have the recipe. Cherish it!

MAKES 1 large round loaf    PREPARATION TIME 10 minutes    COOKING TIME 60 minutes

4 cups flour

I teaspoon salt

I teaspoon baking powder

I teaspoon baking soda

I½-2 cups raisins

⅓ cup plus 2 teaspoons sugar for sprinkling dough

I½ cups buttermilk

2 eggs

⅓ cup butter or vegetable shortening, at room temperature

1. Preheat the oven to 325 degrees.

2. Place flour, salt, baking powder, baking soda, raisins, and ⅓ cup sugar in a large bowl and mix gently with a wooden spoon until well combined. Add the buttermilk, eggs, and butter. Mix and knead until you have slightly sticky dough. This should take about 3 minutes. Form the dough into a ball and place it in a greased, round metal baking dish. Using a sharp knife, cut an X about ¼ inch deep into the dough. Sprinkle the dough with the remaining 2 teaspoons sugar and bake in the preheated oven for 55 to 60 minutes. Cool for 15 minutes, then immediately cover the bread with aluminum foil. I think covering the soda bread after it comes out of the oven was one of Grandma's secrets for keeping her bread so moist. Serve it hot, just warm, or at room temperature.

**Desserts**

# Anise Cookies

I got this recipe from George Feil, one of my longtime massage clients. George was 88 years old, but still drove and was completely independent. He looked like he was in his mid 60s. He made these cookies and the Swedish Butter Cookies (page 168) as a Christmas gift for me and my family one year. We loved them, and George was nice enough to give me his recipes for the cookbook.

MAKES about 60 cookies    PREPARATION TIME 10 minutes
COOKING TIME 10 minutes per batch

½ cup unsalted butter, softened

1 cup sugar

1 teaspoon anise seed, crushed

1 large egg

1 teaspoon cream of tartar

1 teaspoon baking soda

¼ teaspoon salt

2 cups flour

1.  Preheat the oven to 350 degrees.

2.  In a mixing bowl, cream the butter, gradually blending in the sugar. When the mixture is light and fluffy, mix in the anise seed, egg, cream of tartar, baking soda, and salt. When thoroughly combined, add the flour and mix well. Shape level teaspoons of dough into balls and place them on ungreased baking sheets about 2 inches apart. Flatten with the tines of a fork, making a criss-cross pattern. Bake in the preheated oven for 10 minutes until lightly browned. Lift with a spatula onto racks to cool. Store the cookies in a tightly covered tin or container.

# Swedish Butter Cookies

**This is another recipe from George Feil. It dates back to the 1920s, when a friend of the Feil family married a girl from Sweden. It may seem like a lot of cookies, but they're very small and great to give as gifts at holiday time.**

MAKES **about 200 cookies**   PREPARATION TIME **10 minutes**
COOKING TIME **12 to 15 minutes per batch**

6 cups unbleached flour (George preferred Gold Medal)

3 eggs

1 pound butter, at room temperature

2½ cups sugar

1 teaspoon pure vanilla extract

1 teaspoon baking powder

1.  Preheat the oven to 350 degrees.

2.  Thoroughly combine all the ingredients. You can use a cookie press to extrude the dough onto a large cutting board or counter and then cut into 2- to 2½-inch pieces. Lay the cut cookies on a cookie sheet and bake them in batches in the preheated oven for 12 to 15 minutes or until the cookies are slightly brown. Immediately remove them from the pans with a spatula to cool on racks or another tray.

3.  If you don't have a cookie press, roll the dough into the shape of a hot dog bun about 2 inches in diameter and 6 inches long. Wrap it in wax paper and refrigerate it for about 30 minutes to firm up. Cut ¼-inch-thick slices from the dough and place them on the cookie sheet. Press the tines of a fork into the center of the cookies to make a lined impression and bake as above.

Desserts

# Damian's Chocolate-Chip Cookies

By his own account, it took him many attempts to get this recipe just right. He wanted a cookie that remained soft after it cooled, and I think he's achieved his goal. These are soft in the middle and slightly brittle around the edges. When I took a batch to the firehouse, they vanished in seconds. Need I say more?

MAKES approximately 3 dozen    PREPARATION TIME 15 to 20 minutes
COOKING TIME 10 to 12 minutes per batch

> 1 cup (2 sticks) butter
>
> ¼ cup vegetable shortening
>
> ¾ cup brown sugar
>
> ¼ cup granulated sugar
>
> ⅓ cup confectioners' sugar
>
> 1 egg
>
> 2 egg yolks
>
> 1 teaspoon pure vanilla extract
>
> 1¾ cups flour
>
> ½ teaspoon salt
>
> ¼ teaspoon baking soda
>
> 1 (12-ounce) bag chocolate chips

1. Preheat the oven to 350 degrees.

2. In a large bowl, with an electric mixer, cream together the butter, shortening, brown sugar, granulated sugar, and confectioners' sugar until light and fluffy. Add the eggs, yolks, and vanilla and mix gently just to incorporate. Do not overmix. Add the flour, salt, baking soda, and chocolate chips and mix just until the flour is absorbed. Do not overmix.

3. Drop teaspoonfuls of dough onto an ungreased cookie sheet, leaving enough room for the cookies to spread as they bake. Bake on the middle rack of the preheated oven for 10 to 12 minutes. If you prefer a crisper cookie, bake 1 or 2 minutes longer. The bottoms of the cookies should be slightly brown, and the tops very lightly colored. Cool on the cookie sheet.

Desserts

# Italian Ricotta Sfinci

When Damian Ricardella was growing up, he found himself drawn to the kitchen whenever his grandmother was cooking. He says it would have been hard not to get interested in baking with all the cakes, pies, and cookies she always kept in the house. This recipe is one of Damian's favorites. It was one of the first he ever made himself, with his grandma looking over his shoulder. These pastries are light and airy with a golden brown crust coated with cinnamon, sugar, or honey. Damian bets you won't be able to eat just one.

MAKES about 4 dozen     PREPARATION TIME 10 minutes     COOKING TIME 5 to 7 minutes

### BATTER

1 pound ricotta cheese

2 cups flour

5 eggs

4 teaspoons baking powder

2 tablespoons pure vanilla extract

6 teaspoons sugar

6 cups vegetable oil, for deep-frying

### TOPPINGS

1 teaspoon ground cinnamon mixed with ¼ cup sugar, or ½ cup honey and 2 teaspoons pure vanilla extract heated in a small saucepan to thin the honey

In a large bowl, combine all the ingredients for the batter in the order listed and mix until blended. Set the batter aside for 30 minutes. In a large, deep pot, heat the oil to 350 degrees. Carefully drop teaspoonsful of batter into the oil and fry until the sfinci are evenly golden brown. As soon as they are done, transfer them to a bowl and coat immediately with either of the two toppings—or make some of each. Serve immediately.

# Pecan Pie

Pecan pie is one of my favorite desserts. I don't recall ever eating a piece I didn't like. This is Damian Ricardella's recipe and, I promise you, it's amazing. Damian says it's always a big hit around Thanksgiving. From the flaky crust, to the silky smooth custard, to the toasted pecans—for me it's a hit any time.

**SERVES 8  PREPARATION TIME 1½ hours  COOKING TIME 45 minutes**

### FOR THE PIE CRUST

⅔ cup butter

1 cup flour

Pinch of salt

⅓ cup ice-cold water

### FOR THE FILLING

¾ cup granulated sugar

½ cup brown sugar

½ cup honey

½ cup maple syrup

¼ cup dark molasses

5 eggs, beaten

1 cup heavy cream

2 tablespoons butter, melted

1 cup pecans

**TO MAKE THE CRUST:** Cut the butter into 1-inch pieces and refrigerate it. Combine the flour and salt in a mixing bowl and cut in the cold butter to form marble-size pieces. Slowly stir the ice-cold water into the flour mixture; you might not need all the water. Add just enough to moisten the dry ingredients. Once the mixture forms a dough, stop mixing immediately. Wrap the dough in plastic wrap and refrigerate it for at least 1 hour. Preheat the oven to 250 degrees. Roll out the chilled dough on a floured surface to a circle approximately 11 inches in diameter. Spray a 9- or 10-inch pie pan with a nonstick cooking spray. Gently transfer the dough to the pan and press it into the corners. Allow the dough to hang over the edge of the pan approximately half an inch. Fold the excess underneath

Desserts

itself to form a double outer crust on the rim of the pan. With the thumb and forefinger of one hand and the forefinger of the other hand, pinch the double crust into a wavy edge. Place a piece of aluminum foil over the dough and fill it with pie weights or dried beans. Bake in the preheated oven for 15 minutes. Remove the weights and foil and cool the crust for at least 1 hour before filling it.

TO MAKE THE FILLING: Preheat oven to 350 degrees.

In a mixing bowl, combine the granulated sugar, brown sugar, honey, maple syrup, and molasses. Add the eggs and mix just enough to combine. Don't beat air into the eggs, which would create too much foam. If the mixture should become foamy, let it sit for 2 to 4 hours to allow the air to dissipate. Gently stir in the cream. Spread the melted butter and the nuts in the bottom of the prebaked pie crust. Pour the filling mixture over the nuts and bake in the preheated oven until the mixture develops a custardlike consistency, about 45 minutes. When the pan is shaken, the custard should be firm. Don't overbake it or the custard will begin to crack or split. Let the pie cool to room temperature in the pan before cutting and serving.

# Strawberry Cheesecake

Damian says that a good cheesecake recipe is essential to any pastry chef's repertoire. He believes that a slice of this, served with a strong cup of coffee, is one of the best ways to complete a great meal. If you remove the cake from the refrigerator 15 to 20 minutes before serving, it will have a creamier consistency.

SERVES **8 to 10**    PREPARATION TIME **40 minutes**    COOKING TIME **1 hour, 10 minutes**

### FOR THE FILLING

**1 (20-ounce) package frozen strawberries**

**1 cup sugar**

### FOR THE CRUST

**2 wrapped "stacks" from a box of graham crackers**

**3 tablespoons brown sugar**

**1 tablespoon butter, melted**

**1 large egg white**

### FOR THE CAKE

**1½ pounds cream cheese, at room temperature**

**¾ cup sugar**

**⅔ cup sour cream**

**4 egg yolks**

**3 whole eggs**

**¼ cup heavy cream**

**2½ teaspoons pure vanilla extract**

**1½ teaspoons freshly squeezed lemon juice**

TO MAKE THE FILLING: Allow the berries to defrost slightly, then transfer them to a small saucepan along with the sugar. Set the pan over medium heat until the mixture starts to simmer. Lower the heat and simmer until the mixture is thickened, about 15 to 20 minutes. Remove from the heat and cool to room temperature for 10 minutes, then transfer to the freezer for 20 minutes to finish cooling and thicken slightly. While you're waiting for the filling to cool, prepare the crust.

Desserts

**TO MAKE THE CRUST:** Preheat the oven to 350 degrees.

Grind the graham crackers and brown sugar together in a food processor. You'll need 1½ cups ground crumbs. Transfer the crumbs to a mixing bowl. Add the melted butter and mix well. Add the egg white and mix well again. To test for proper moistness, squeeze some of the crumbs in your hand, if the mixture forms a ball, it's moist enough; if not, add another egg white. Lightly grease a 9-inch cake pan, spread the crumbs on the bottom, and pack down tightly. Bake the crust in the preheated oven for 5 to 8 minutes.

**TO MAKE THE CHEESECAKE:** Soften the cream cheese with a handheld electric mixer or the paddle attachment of a large standing kitchen mixer. Add the sugar and beat until smooth. Scrape the bottom of the bowl to be sure there are no lumps of cream cheese remaining. Add the sour cream and beat until light and airy. Scrape the bottom of the bowl again to make sure there are no lumps before you begin adding the eggs, because once the eggs are added the lumps will not come out. Add the yolks and beat until fully incorporated. Beat in the whole eggs slowly, allowing the mixture to absorb them. Add the heavy cream, vanilla, and lemon juice and mix thoroughly.

**TO ASSEMBLE AND BAKE THE CAKE:** Preheat the oven to 350. Spread half the filling evenly over the precooked crust. Pour the cheesecake batter over the filling. Randomly dot the remaining strawberry mixture onto the batter and swirl it with the spoon. You might not use it all. Place the cake pan inside a larger roasting or baking pan and put it in the pre-heated oven. Carefully pour water into the larger pan to a depth of ½ inch. Bake for approximately 1 hour, 10 minutes or until the center feels soft but set. Check from time to time to be sure there is still water in the outer pan. If not, add more; otherwise, the cheesecake will brown. Cool the cheesecake in its pan on a wire rack until it is just semi-warm. Then refrigerate for at least 8 hours or overnight.

**TO REMOVE THE CAKE FROM THE PAN,** Place the pan over low heat on the stovetop to warm the bottom slightly. Place a piece of plastic wrap on top of the cheesecake, and invert a 10-inch plate on top of the plastic. Keeping one hand over the plate and the other under the pan, flip the cheesecake to remove it from the pan. It will be upside-down. Leaving the cake on the plastic, transfer the plate to the top (actually the bottom) of the cake, flip it right side up, and remove the plastic. Cut the cake with a warm, wet knife to make clean slices.

# Mississippi Mud

If you are not a chocolate enthusiast, just keep turning the pages. This is a rich, chocolaty, gooey concoction that will satisfy any chocoholic's sweet tooth—it might even cure it. For best results, the cakes should be baked a day in advance and refrigerated until you're ready to assemble the dessert.

SERVES 10    PREPARATION TIME 20 minutes    COOKING TIME 20 to 25 minutes

### FOR THE CAKES

¾ pound (3 sticks) butter

3 cups sugar

9 eggs

3 teaspoons pure vanilla extract

2¼ cups flour

1 teaspoon salt

1 cup cocoa powder

2½ teaspoons baking powder

½ cup semi-sweet chocolate chips

### FOR THE GANACHE

½ cup semi-sweet chocolate chips

⅓ cup heavy cream

TO MAKE THE CAKES: Preheat the oven to 350 degrees. Grease a 9-inch round cake pan and a medium sheet pan.

IN AN ELECTRIC MIXER, using the paddle attachment, cream the butter and sugar until the mixture is light and fluffy. Slowly add the eggs, one at a time, mixing well after each addition. Mix in the vanilla. Sift together the flour, salt, cocoa powder, and baking powder. Add the dry ingredients and chocolate chips to the butter and eggs and mix to lightly incorporate the flour. Remove the paddle and continue to fold by hand until all the flour is absorbed. Fill the prepared pan halfway with the batter. Spread the remaining batter on a sheet pan. Cook both cakes in the preheated oven for approximately 20 minutes. Test the 9-inch cake with an instant-read thermometer; it should be between 140 and 145 degrees and the center should be gooey. Bake the cake on the sheet pan until a

Desserts

toothpick inserted comes out clean. Allow both cakes to cool thoroughly, either in their pans or on a rack.

**TO MAKE THE GANACHE:** Put the chocolate chips in a bowl. Bring the heavy cream to a boil in a small pan and pour over the chocolate chips. Let the mixture sit for 1 minute to soften the chocolate, then stir to melt all the chocolate.

**TO ASSEMBLE THE DESSERT:** Remove the 9-inch cake from its pan and put it on a cake platter. Melt the ganache in a double boiler. Cut the sheet cake into cubes. Spread a thin layer of ganache over the top of the round cake so the cubes will adhere to it. Pile the cubes on top of the cake any which way. Drizzle ganache over the cubes and refrigerate to set the ganache. Before serving, warm each slice in the microwave to warm the center. For true decadence, serve it "a la mode" with vanilla ice cream.

# Flan

This is another of Damian Ricardella's delightful recipes and a favorite dessert of mine. The custard is velvety smooth, and the caramel sauce is decadently sweet.

SERVES **8 to 10**   PREPARATION TIME **30 minutes**   COOKING TIME **45 minutes**

### FOR THE CUSTARD

**2 cups whole milk**

**4 eggs**

**½ cup egg yolks (approximately 4 to 6, depending on the size of the eggs)**

**I cup sugar**

**Pinch of salt**

**I teaspoon pure vanilla extract**

### FOR THE CARAMEL SAUCE

**1½ cups sugar**

**¼ cup water (enough to moisten the sugar)**

### FOR THE GARNISH:

**I cup heavy cream, whipped with 4 tablespoons sugar and I teaspoon pure vanilla extract**

**I pint berries of your choice**

TO MAKE THE CUSTARD: Warm the milk to a simmer but do not boil and set it aside. In a mixing bowl, combine the eggs, yolks, sugar, and salt. Slowly add the milk to the egg mixture, stirring constantly with a whisk to avoid cooking the eggs. Stir in the vanilla, cover, and set aside.

TO MAKE THE SAUCE: Combine the sugar and water in a clean, heavy-bottomed saucepan with a lid. Stir to make sure all the sugar is moistened; if there is any dry sugar, add a bit more water and stir again. With wet fingers, wipe off all the excess sugar from the sides of the pan to prevent it from crystallizing. Cover the pan and cook on medium-high heat without stirring until the sugar reaches 240 degrees on a candy thermometer or when it starts to become slightly thick. This will take approximately 5 to 7 minutes. Remove the cover and continue cooking until the caramel turns light brown. Remove the pan from the heat and immediately place the pot in an ice water bath until the bubbling stops, about 30 seconds. *Do not touch the sugar.* Be extremely careful when you cook sugar; it can burn you very badly.

TO COOK THE FLAN: Preheat the oven to 350 degrees. Carefully ladle the caramelized sugar into 8 to 10 individual ramekins or a 9-inch round baking dish. (If the sugar starts to harden while you're pouring it, just return the pan to the heat until it softens and start to ladle again.) Allow the sugar to cool enough to harden, then pour in the custard. Set the ramekins or baking dish in a larger roasting or baking pan, and place the sheet pan in the oven. Carefully pour water into the outer pan to come halfway up the sides of the ramekins or baking dish. The flan is done cooking when you shake the baking dish and the center does not appear to be liquid, about 45 minutes. Remove from the water bath and cool. Then refrigerate overnight. To remove the flan from the dish or ramekins, run a small knife around the edge. Place a serving dish (with a lip to catch the caramel sauce) over the flan. Flip the flan over and tap the serving dish on the counter to allow flan to drop onto the dish. Garnish with the sweetened whipped cream and berries.

## Class Trips

**From time to time during the school year, class trips are scheduled to different firehouses around the city. Usually the kids are bused to the one that's nearest their school. These trips are great for the kids but can be a logistical nightmare for the firefighters.**

**Generally, it's the junior men and probies who are in charge. We have to contain the children within a certain area and hold their attention as we talk to them about fire safety. We've got to keep it interesting and light so they can interact with us and learn what to do in case a fire breaks out in their home or apartment. The probies also put on their bunker gear and masks and crawl around the children, so the kids won't be afraid to come to us in case they're caught in a fire. This is usually the time when some of the children start to cry because we do look kind of scary.**

**If a call comes in while the children are climbing in and out of the rig, we have to move them quickly and safely out of our quarters while we dress and respond. This is where things can get a little bit hairy, because it definitely wouldn't look good if we responded to a call with a small child on top of the apparatus.**

# Smoldering Crème Brûlée

In 2001 I entered Tabasco's Nationwide Cook and Ladder Competition and was lucky enough to win second place, which was $5,000—$2,500 for me and $2,500 for my firehouse. I had a great time and definitely would have entered again in 2002, but this time Tabasco determined that I wasn't eligible because I'd had "previous culinary experience." The dish I had made, Shrimp Cordon Bleu with Mushroom, Cognac, and Tabasco Sauce, was so complicated that total strangers were calling me at home to vent their frustration, which is why I haven't included it in this book. Anyway, just because I couldn't enter didn't mean that my good friend Dave McAndrews couldn't submit a recipe I'd kind of helped him with, right? We came up with this Smoldering Crème Brûlée, and Dave did an excellent job cooking in the competition even though we—I mean he—didn't place. It was still a lot of fun, and we got to meet some great firefighters from across the country.

SERVES 8    PREPARATION TIME 15 minutes    COOKING TIME 30 to 35 minutes

Dave "Dirtball" McAndrews, me, and Paul Miller at the 2002 Tabasco Cook and Ladder competition

## FOR THE CUSTARD

**4 cups heavy cream**

**I teaspoon pure vanilla extract**

**I½ teaspoons Tabasco original (optional)**

**8 egg yolks**

**½ cup sugar**

## FOR THE TOPPING

**I teaspoon sugar per ramekin, or if you are using a single baking dish, ¼ cup**

1. Position the rack in the center of the oven and preheat the oven to 300 degrees.

2. Fill a medium saucepan ¾ full with water and place it over high heat to come to a boil.

3. Warm the cream, vanilla, and Tabasco sauce (if using) in a medium saucepan over medium-low heat until bubbles start to form around the edge and steam begins to rise from the surface. Remove from the heat and set aside.

4. In a medium-size bowl, whisk the egg yolks and sugar together until the mixture turns a pale yellow, about 3 minutes. Slowly combine the warm cream with the egg yolks.

5. Divide the mixture among 8 (6-ounce) ramekins or pour it into one medium-size baking dish. Set the ramekins into a larger pan, set it on the oven rack, and carefully pour in the boiling water until it comes halfway up the sides of the ramekins. Cook the custard for 35 minutes.

6. Transfer the custard(s) to an ice-filled baking pan and refrigerate for at least 2 hours.

7. To serve, sprinkle the custard(s) with the topping sugar and use a kitchen torch to melt to a golden perfection. If you don't have a torch, you can put the crème brûlée under the broiler for a minute to melt the sugar—but watch it very carefully! Serve immediately.

# Muligooch's Rice Pudding

The guys at my firehouse love it when Jimmy Mulligan, L-156, makes his mother-in-law Henrietta's rice pudding. What I like about it is the loose consistency, which is the way I think rice pudding should be. The recipe is great as it is, but you can also vary it by using the suggestions below.

SERVES 8 to 10    PREPARATION TIME 5 minutes    COOKING TIME about 1 hour

   2 quarts whole milk

   ¾ cup long grain white rice

   2 eggs

   ¾ cup sugar

   1 teaspoon ground cinnamon, for garnish

1.  Warm (do not boil) the milk in a large saucepan. Add the rice and cook over a medium heat, stirring constantly, for 25 to 30 minutes.

2.  Combine the eggs and sugar in a mixing bowl and whisk in 1 cup milk from the rice pot. After 30 minutes, add the egg and sugar mixture to the rice and cook 30 minutes more, stirring frequently. Remove the pudding from the heat and transfer it to a serving dish. Sprinkle with the cinnamon, cool for about 30 minutes at room temperature, then refrigerate for at least 1 hour before serving.

Variations:

   1. Mix 1 cup raisins into the cooked pudding.

   2. Add 1 teaspoon pure vanilla extract to the rice along with the egg and sugar mixture.

   3. Damian Ricardella recommends adding 1 cup dried cranberries and some grated lemon zest along with the eggs and sugar.

   4. Mix in 1 cup dried cherries and 1 teaspoon pure vanilla extract when you add the eggs and sugar.

Desserts

# John Sineno's Famous No-Bake Rice Pudding

**Every member of the FDNY who's been on the job for any length of time knows John Sineno. When I asked him if he would allow me to use one of his recipes in my cookbook, he graciously said, "Whatever I can do to help you." All the firemen I know love his rice pudding, so here it is. This recipe is from *The New Firefighter's Cookbook*.**

SERVES 20

I pound long-grain rice

I gallon whole milk

3 cups sugar

3 ounces vanilla extract

2 (12-ounce) cans evaporated milk

I package vanilla tapioca pudding

5 eggs, beaten

Raisins (optional; as many or few as you want)

Ground cinnamon, for garnish

In a large saucepan with a lid, cook the rice, milk, and sugar, stirring occasionally, until the mixture comes to a slow boil. Reduce the heat and let it simmer—and remember, stirring prevents the mixture from sticking. As the mixture begins to thicken, add the vanilla, evaporated milk, and tapioca pudding. Stir well and cover. Very slowly and gradually, add the eggs to the simmering mixture. Cook, stirring, until thickened. If raisins are to be added, place in a bowl, cover with boiling water, and let stand 15 minutes and drain. Put the raisins in the bottom of a large baking pan (or two disposable foil baking pans); pour the pudding over the raisins, stir, and then let the mixture cool. Sprinkle the top of the rice pudding with cinnamon before serving.

John Sineno E-58, FDNY, retired

# John Sineno and the History of Cooking in the Firehouse

When my publisher asked me one day why we associate firefighters with food, I said I thought it had a lot to do with one man, John Sineno, of E-58, who was the author of two of the first firefighter's cookbooks ever published.

John got on the job with the FDNY on October 2, 1962, and the first question his captain asked him was, "Do you cook?" Luckily, he'd had some catering experience and was able to say "Yes." When he saw how the kitchen was set up, however, he realized it was not conducive to doing much cooking. There was a four-burner electric stovetop and two companies (a total of 14 men) to feed. The electric elements sometimes worked and sometimes didn't, but the guys at the firehouse made do.

John told me that most of the men "brown-bagged" their meals in those days, and when I asked him what they brought, he said, "Usually a quart of Ballantine Ale."

During a recent conversation, John recalled cooking during the Harlem riots in the 1960s. He didn't go home for four days and nights during which he cooked for countless numbers of men from his battalion, and even for the cops. Firemen would show up in teams, and John would feed them like clockwork. He went out to shop each morning and cleaned out stores of their roasts, frozen vegetables, and potatoes. Then he went back to the firehouse with his sup-

John "Mama" Sineno giving Meg Bowles and me some cooking tips

plies and cooked all afternoon and evening, taking care of the guys with fresh food whenever they arrived. After that, he became affectionately known as "Mama Sineno" in his firehouse because he always made sure everyone had something to eat.

John's first big taste of recognition came when he won first prize at an **FDNY** cheesecake competition in 1984. That got him an appearance on *Donahue*. After his segment, Donahue pulled John aside and told him he should write a cookbook. Then he actually followed through with an introduction to a publisher, and things just took off from there. *The Firefighter's Cookbook,* published in 1986, was a collection of recipes from different firefighters and their wives. John gave half the proceeds to The Burn Center established at Cornell Medical Center.

He retired from the **FDNY** in 1990, after 28 years of service but was still able to publish a second cookbook, *The New Firefighter's Cookbook,* in 1996. John gave all the proceeds from the new book to FDNY fraternal clubs' college scholarship funds in his son Thomas's name because, he said, he wanted to help provide kids who might be having problems with some direction. If he helped only a couple kids, he told me, he'd consider it a home run.

Many people have seen John Sineno on TV or heard about him through the department. He and his cookbooks are definitely among the most important reasons the public now associates firefighters with food, and if it weren't for him, it's quite possible you wouldn't be reading this book right now.

John passed away on April 2, 2003, and many people, including me and all firefighters, will miss him.

# What Every Kitchen Should Have

## Pots and Pans

STAINLESS-STEEL POTS AND PANS I recommend these especially for the home. I'm talking here about heavy-duty pots and pans with an aluminum core for heat conduction and a $\frac{1}{180}$-inch thick stainless-steel covering. The lids and handles are also made of stainless steel, and the handles should be bolted on, not merely spot-welded. These pans will last you a lifetime. Don't buy pots with plastic, screwed-in handles because you won't be able to put them in the oven. The All Clad brand is top of the line, but I have a set of Kirkland pots and pans, which are sold at Costco or the Price Club for a quarter the price of All Clad, and they are every bit as good, if not better. In fact, the Kirkland lids are actually thicker and sturdier than the All Clad.

JERRY RUOTOLO

Speaking to the students at New York Technical College about quality ingredients

Stainless steel is a nonreactive metal, which means that if you use a stainless-steel spoon for mixing, or you're cooking something acidic like a tomato sauce, it will not react with the metal as it would if you were using an aluminum pan.

If you are using aluminum pans, I suggest that you use only wooden spoons for mixing so you don't scrape any aluminum into your food.

CAST-IRON POTS AND PANS The only thing I wouldn't cook in a cast-iron pan is tomato sauce, which is acidic and might react with the pan, but everything else is fair game. I have one cast-iron Dutch oven at home and one 10-inch skillet, and I love them both.

At the firehouse we have two 12-inch skillets and one 5½-quart Dutch oven for frying. The guys have really grown attached to these.

TEFLON PANS I use these only for cooking eggs, *nothing else*. Eggs are effortless to cook and a pleasure to flip in a well-heated Teflon pan. I suggest an 8- or 10-inch skillet for this. And please remember, *never* use metal utensils with a Teflon pan, because it scratches so easily. If you are using a scratched-up Teflon pan, toss it out.

There are heat-resistant plastic utensils made especially for use with Teflon pans.

SHEET PANS At the firehouse we use full sheet pans, and at home I use half-sheet pans. A sheet pan is basically an aluminum cookie sheet with a 1-inch lip. You can use them for everything from baking cookies to roasting meats or poultry. They come in full or half size. Your choice will depend on the quantity of food you need to cook as well as the size of your oven.

PYREX OR CERAMIC BAKING DISHES These are great for desserts such as flan or crème brûlée, as well as for stuffings and for reheating food in the microwave.

## Utensils

KNIVES Knives are among the most important tools you'll ever use in a kitchen. You need a decent set for the firehouse and a great set for your home. For the firehouse, I purchased a few 8- and 10-inch chef's knives. We also have a couple offset serrated knives, which are great for onions, tomatoes, bread, and sandwiches. At home I have a small collection of Wusthof Classic knives.

One of the most important things to consider when purchasing good-quality knives is how they fit and feel in your hand. If the handle feels too thick or too small, keep looking. Good-quality knives are expensive, but you'll have them a lifetime if you care for them properly, so make sure they feel comfortable to hold. Along with your knives, you'll need a good steel. A steel does not actually sharpen the blade but removes the burrs that dull the edge.

TONGS These are an extension of your hands that make it easy to turn and grab food in a pot or pan.

ROASTING FORKS These are great for lifting a heavy roast or turkey from the pan as well as for checking temperatures on meats. The fork should have tines that are curved so that whatever you're lifting doesn't slide off.

HEAT-RESISTANT PLASTIC UTENSILS Plastic utensils are perfect for use on Teflon pans. Oxo is the brand I like. They're made of sturdy black plastic with matching ergonomic handles and are built to last.

HEAT-RESISTANT RUBBER SPATULA These are great for getting all the batter out of a mixing bowl as well as stirring scrambled eggs. Which brand? Oxo again.

WOODEN SPOONS Wooden utensils can be used on any surface without scratching it. I love to use them for sautéing veggies or making a marinara sauce. You can't go wrong with wood.

## Other Essentials

OVEN THERMOMETER Once you start using an oven thermometer, you'll realize just how valuable a tool it really is. I didn't actually begin to use one until I was writing this book. I found out that my very own brand-new oven was 35 degrees hotter than the temperature for which it was set. That's a lot, and, particularly if you're baking, a difference of 35 degrees one way or the other can make the difference between delicious and disaster.

After I made that discovery, I also bought an oven thermometer for the firehouse. That oven, I discovered, was 50 degrees hotter than the mark. So take my advice, a $12 investment can save you a lot of heartache in the kitchen.

INSTANT-READ MEAT THERMOMETER This is a really great tool particularly for the novice or intermediate cook. If you don't cook roasts or steaks on a daily basis, this little gadget can really help you out. It's about the size of a pen, with a 1-inch instant-read dial thermometer on the top. You stick it in the thickest part of the meat when you think it's nearing the end of its cooking time and the dial moves up to tell you the internal temperature. The dials are also marked to tell you the correct internal temperature for different kinds of meat cooked "medium."

As you use the thermometer, you can also practice getting a feel for the doneness of roasts. First use the thermometer. Then, when you have a read on the temperature, pierce the meat with a roasting fork and hold the fork against your lips. If the roast is medium rare (125 degrees on the thermometer), the fork will feel just a bit warmer than your skin.

You should also begin to get a feel for the resistance of the roast by pressing it with your fingers. Rare meat will have plenty of give. At medium you'll notice the meat is a little firmer. At well done the meat won't have much give at all.

I like to cook meat on the rare side because you can always return it to the oven, but once you've overcooked it, there is no turning back. Here are a few temperatures to use as a guide:

| | |
|---|---|
| RED MEATS | 120F—rare |
| | 125F—medium rare |
| | 130F—medium |
| | 135F—medium well |
| | 140F—well done |
| PORK OR VEAL | 140F—medium |
| | 150F—well done |

BOX CHEESE GRATER These are great for shredding cheese or carrots, zesting lemons or limes, or grating fresh hard Romano or Parmesan cheese.

CITRUS JUICER At a cost of just about $5, this gadget makes it a little bit easier to extract the juice from lemons and limes.

COLANDERS AND SIEVES These are necessary for draining pasta or vegetables and for removing lumps from gravies.

MANUAL CAN OPENER I like to open cans by hand, and, in any case, a manual can opener takes up less space in the kitchen. Oxo is my favorite brand for this, too, because the handle is soft and ergonomic and makes can-opening a breeze.

VEGETABLE PEELER You really need one of these to peel potatoes or vegetables so you don't wind up throwing out too much of the good stuff with the peel. I like the Oxo brand for this also.

STAINLESS-STEEL MIXING BOWLS Stainless steel because they are non-reactive and non-breakable.

**CUTTING BOARDS** Always cut, slice, and chop on a board. You'll be extending the life of your knives as well as the life of your countertop.

Keep one board specifically for cutting raw poultry, and be sure to scrub it thoroughly with soap and hot water after each use.

**FOOD PROCESSOR** It purées, chops, dices, and grinds, and makes chopping fresh garlic a lot easier for the guys at the firehouse.

**BLENDER** I use my blender quite frequently. It's great for everything from puréeing soups to making protein shakes or pesto. I also use it to chop the tomatoes for my marinara sauce. One day, when I have a little more space, I'm going to purchase an immersion blender; that way I won't even have to remove the soup from the pot to blend it.

**GOOD QUALITY PEPPER GRINDER** There is nothing quite like the taste of freshly ground pepper in your favorite salad or pasta dish. Some pepper grinders are mediocre and some are fantastic—go for the fantastic ones. Try to shop at a reputable store that has them on display and will allow you try them before purchasing one.

**OVEN MITTS** So you don't burn your beautiful hands. Try not to get them wet before picking up a hot pan so you don't wind up with a nice steam burn.

**FIRE EXTINGUISHER** The ABC classification is the best because it works for trash, wood, paper, grease, liquids, and electrical fires.

Do not place the extinguisher near the oven, because if you have a stove or oven fire you won't be able to reach it when you need it. The best placement is near an exit from the kitchen where you can grab it and try to extinguish the fire before you leave and call the fire department.

JERRY RUOTOLO

Leaving our boots in our bunker pants makes them a lot easier to jump into when a call comes in

# Index

Page numbers in *italics* indicate photographs; those in **bold** indicate tables.

Made in the USA
Middletown, DE
21 December 2018